# *T. S. Eliot*

## MOMENTS AND PATTERNS

### by Leonard Unger

UNIVERSITY OF MINNESOTA PRESS, Minneapolis

PRINTED IN THE UNITED STATES OF AMERICA AT THE
NORTH CENTRAL PUBLISHING CO., ST. PAUL

3

*Library of Congress Catalog Card Number: 66-27420*

Second printing 1967

PUBLISHED IN GREAT BRITAIN, INDIA, AND PAKISTAN BY THE OXFORD
UNIVERSITY PRESS, LONDON, BOMBAY, AND KARACHI, AND IN CANADA BY THE
COPP CLARK PUBLISHING CO. LIMITED, TORONTO

*for* S. G. U.
"It's strange that words are so inadequate."

# Acknowledgments

TWO of the essays included here were written during periods of residence at Yaddo, so I welcome this chance to express my gratitude to the Corporation of Yaddo and to Mrs. Elizabeth Ames.

Besides the persons mentioned in the Introduction, many others, over a period of many years, have encouraged and helped me toward the writing of these essays. If I do not name them here it is not only because they are numerous, but also because I might recall, too late and with regret, one or two whom I had failed to name.

"The Intimate Voice" first appeared in the *Southern Review*, "Images of Awareness" in the *Sewanee Review*. The editors of these publications have kindly granted permission for reprinting the essays here.

For permission to quote from poems and plays by T. S. Eliot, I am grateful to Harcourt, Brace & World, Inc., Farrar, Straus & Giroux, Inc., and Faber & Faber, Ltd.

L. U.

# Contents

INTRODUCTION                                3

T. S. ELIOT'S MAGIC LANTERN                 7

ASH WEDNESDAY                              41

THE ROSE-GARDEN                            69

ELIOT'S CRITICS                            92

LAFORGUE, CONRAD, AND ELIOT               103

THE INTIMATE VOICE                        157

IMAGES OF AWARENESS                       161

SELECTED BIBLIOGRAPHY                     189

INDEX                                     193

*T. S. Eliot*

MOMENTS AND PATTERNS

# Introduction

IN THINKING about what I might say in this Introduction, my thoughts have turned not only to Eliot and his poetry, but also to the fact that I have written these essays. They were written not as a planned and single effort, but on various occasions over a period of almost three decades.

My first engagement with Eliot's poetry, beyond reading it, was to give a brief report on a passage from *Ash Wednesday* when I was an undergraduate in John Crowe Ransom's class at Vanderbilt University. At the time this seemed like a bright thing to do. Few, if any, of my classmates had heard of the poem. In addition to the pleasure of appearing bright to Mr. Ransom and myself, I was by that time genuinely enthralled by Eliot's poetry. About a year later, when I was a graduate student at Louisiana State University, I elaborated my report for Ransom into a short paper for Cleanth Brooks. This led to conversations between student and teacher, and to my lucky decision to write a Master's thesis, under Brooks's supervision, on *Ash Wednesday*. Brooks had recently published his explication of *The Waste Land*. It was on his advice that I read St. John of the Cross and various other writers whose work provided clarifications of Eliot's poem. At that time Eliot was considered a questionable subject for a graduate

3

thesis, but it was possible for me to do it because I had the support of Brooks, and of his colleague Robert Penn Warren.

Everything else that I have written on Eliot has followed from the experience of exploring *Ash Wednesday* — for indeed the preparation of the thesis was an experience of exploration. It was an education beyond anything else I had encountered in academic routines. I had grabbed hold of something, and it moved, and I hung on. This is what it felt like, too, to write the other essays on Eliot's poetry. In none of the essays have I praised Eliot for providing me with such exercise and such sensation, so I am happy to do so here.

The thesis was written in the spring of 1938, and the essay on *Ash Wednesday* was adapted from it in the summer of that year. By the time I completed the essay, I was aware of the childhood experience in the rose garden as a persistent and developing theme throughout Eliot's poetry and plays. But I did not get around to writing "The Rose Garden" until the summer of 1941, after I had completed my graduate studies at the State University of Iowa.

The essay called "Eliot's Critics" was written in 1947 as an Introduction to *T. S. Eliot: A Selected Critique,* a collection of comment on Eliot by thirty-one different writers. I undertook preparing the volume as a means of getting back to my own work and my own interests, after having served with the armed forces during World War II.

The year of original publication is given at the end of each essay. "T. S. Eliot's Magic Lantern" has been placed at the opening of the book because it was written as a general introduction to Eliot's work. The other essays are arranged in the order in which I wrote them, for I believe that this arrangement gives them a natural and essential continuity. The arrangement is also relevant to the fact that I have preferred to make no over-all revisions, no effort to bring the essays up-to-date, for there is a sense in which each essay belongs to the time it was written. That, too, is a part of the continuity. But I have made editorial changes at a number of points for various reasons. For example, "T. S. Eliot's Magic Lantern" (which was originally a pamphlet called *T. S. Eliot*) has been shortened by several pages in order to avoid repetition with some of the other essays.

The most substantial and interesting change was made in "Laforgue, Conrad, and Eliot." In that essay, as I opened the discussion of Conrad, I quoted from *Heart of Darkness* the sentence which is echoed in *The Waste Land*: "In the offing the sea and the sky were welded together without a joint, and in the luminous space the tanned sails of the barges drifting up with the tide seemed to stand still in red clusters of canvas sharply peaked, with gleams of varnished sprits." However — in the edition of Conrad which I was using, the last word was printed (rather, misprinted) "spirits." Either I assumed that this should be "vanished spirits" or else I actually read it that way. This reading fitted beautifully the idea I was developing and I made the most of it. Only a few paragraphs later in *Heart of Darkness* Conrad speaks of "the great spirit of the past," and I was hot enough on the trail of an idea to associate "past" and "vanished." Fortunately, the error merely fitted into an already determined and valid pattern, so I was able to correct the error with no difficulty or distortion.

Although I have a wisp of regret that Conrad had not actually written "vanished spirits," it has been gratifying to correct the error. I have been pleased also to make another change in the essay, a change for which I am indebted to T. S. Eliot himself. I had first used some passages from Laforgue's prose tale "Hamlet" translated by Francis Newman, and these are now replaced with the translation given by Arthur Symons in the chapter on Laforgue in his book *The Symbolist Movement in Literature*. In a letter graciously thanking me for a copy of my book *The Man in the Name*, Eliot said that he thought Symons' translation was clearer and more accurate, and it is. It is also more meaningful to quote Symons, since it is well known that it was his book which introduced Eliot to Laforgue — to whom Eliot was indebted "more than to any one poet in any language," as Eliot said so recently as 1961.

The last two essays, "The Intimate Voice" and "Images of Awareness," were written (in that order) as Tributes in the months immediately following Eliot's death. Anyone reading the essays may see that they have a special relation to each other, for the later essay is in some respects an elaboration of matters briefly treated in the earlier. I could say, as a common footnote to both essays, that the "intimate voice" of Eliot's poetry is an "image of awareness." While writing "Images of Awareness" I came to realize that there is a special relation also with my earlier essay "Fusion and Experience," where I examine Eliot's famous critical dictum that English metaphysical poetry is marked by a "fusion of thought and feeling." My common footnote here would be that Eliot's own "images of awareness" illustrate something of what he meant by the "fusion of thought and feeling." Readers who are interested in this subject are referred to my book *The Man in the Name*, where the earlier essay may be found. I have not included "Fusion and Experience" here because it is primarily about the literary criticism of Eliot and a number of other critics.

In looking back on these essays, I have been struck (but not surprised) by the fact that five of them — all but those on *Ash Wednesday* and Eliot's critics — are concerned with details selected in each case from the larger body of Eliot's poetry, as well as from the plays, and even the criticism. It is this consideration which led me to choose *Moments and Patterns* as the title of my book. It appears that I have been drawn to write about Eliot's poetry when I became aware that one or another set of details selected from Eliot's work yielded a pattern. Such patterns are interwoven with each other and are finally to be seen as parts of that larger pattern which is the entire work. Eliot was preoccupied with form, not as something ready at hand, but as something to be pursued. This is what makes his work so emphatically modern. It is still modern. The form of his work is a form which has not been completed. It required an arduous effort to produce a form that remains open, that reaches at some points, at some moments, the frontier of the unexplored. The poet's life is closed, but in his work "the pattern is new in every moment." *Four Quartets* dwells throughout on this subject of moments and patterns, and it is this fact, too, which suggested the title.

*1966*

6

# T. S. Eliot's Magic Lantern

## I

"I PERCEIVED that I myself had always been a New Englander in the South West [meaning St. Louis, Missouri], and a South Westerner in New England." This comment of T. S. Eliot's, referring to his childhood and youth in the United States, was published in 1928 — a year after he had become an English subject and had entered the Church of England. About thirty years later, in an interview conducted in New York, he affirmed that his poetry belongs in the tradition of American literature: "I'd say that my poetry has obviously more in common with my distinguished contemporaries in America, than with anything written in my generation in England. That I'm sure of." To the question whether there was "a connection with the American past," he answered: "Yes, but I couldn't put it any more definitely than that, you see. It wouldn't be what it is, and I imagine it wouldn't be so good; putting it as modestly as I can, it wouldn't be what it is if I'd been born in England, and it wouldn't be what it is if I'd stayed in America. It's a combination of things. But in its sources, in its emotional springs, it comes from America." *

*The interview from which this and other statements are quoted was conducted by Donald Hall and appears in the *Paris Review*, Number 21 (Spring–Summer 1959).

7

The poet's parents were both descended from old New England families. His paternal grandfather had come to St. Louis from Harvard Divinity School to establish the city's first Unitarian church and then to found and preside over Washington University. His father, Henry Ware Eliot, became president of a local industry, the Hydraulic Press Brick Company of St. Louis. His mother, Charlotte Chauncey Stearns, was the author of a long poem on the life of Savonarola and an extended biography of her father-in-law. Thomas Stearns Eliot, the youngest of seven children, was born September 26, 1888. In his own words, the Eliot family in St. Louis "guarded jealously its connexions with New England."

After attending the Smith Academy in St. Louis, Eliot completed his preparation for college at the Milton Academy in Massachusetts and then entered Harvard in the fall of 1906, where he pursued philosophy as his major field of study. As an undergraduate he edited and contributed poems to the *Harvard Advocate*. He completed the college course in three years and then continued to study philosophy in the Graduate School, with an interruption for one year's study (1910–11) at the Sorbonne. In 1914 he returned to Europe, studying first in Germany and then, after the outbreak of the war, at Oxford. Although he completed a doctoral dissertation on the philosophy of F. H. Bradley, he never returned to Harvard for formal acceptance of the degree. After marrying Miss Vivienne Haigh Haigh-Wood in 1915, Eliot was employed briefly as a teacher of various subjects at a boy's school near London, and after that at Lloyds Bank. A physical condition prevented him from entering the United States Navy in 1918. From 1917 to 1919 he was assistant editor of the *Egoist*, and for that period and the years immediately following, besides writing poetry, he supported himself by writing for magazines and periodicals reviews and essays, some of which have since become famous. Eliot's personal literary relations led him into the publishing business — eventually to become a director of Faber and Faber. He became editor of the *Criterion* at its outset in 1922, a quarterly review which played an important part in literary developments for the period of its duration. (It ceased publication, by Eliot's decision, at the approach of World War II.) After an absence of eighteen years, he returned to the United States in order to give the Charles Eliot Norton lectures at Harvard in 1932–33. He made increasingly frequent visits to his native country, lecturing and giving readings at various institutions, and accepting official awards of honor. The British Order of Merit and the Nobel Prize for Literature were awarded to him in 1948, and other distinctions of international eminence followed. In 1947 his first wife died, after prolonged illness and residence in a nursing home. In January of 1957 he married Miss Valerie Fletcher, who had been his private secretary.

It would be too crudely simple to regard the divided regional identity of Eliot's youth as the cause of qualities which have characterized his thought and work. But this early dual identity does prefigure and illustrate a large and inclusive pattern. Eliot was both Westerner and New Englander, but not wholly one or the other. So with his migration to England and Englishness. In his early literary criticism, the prose of the twenties and thirties, there are sometimes tones and gestures which out-English the English as only a foreigner, and perhaps only an American, could do. In religion he became a "Catholic" and an apologist for Catholicism, but he was not a Roman Catholic. His criticism urged a program of the classical, the traditional, and the impersonal, while he was producing a poetry which is poignantly romantic, strikingly modernist, and intensely personal. When others protested that there was a marked contradiction between his theory and his practice, Eliot explained: "In one's prose reflexions one may be legitimately occupied with ideals, whereas in the writing of verse one can only deal with actuality." And yet, in the later stages of his career Eliot frequently referred to the intimate relation between his prose — especially the discussions of specific poets — and his own poetry. Of that kind of criticism — which he has called "workshop criticism" — he said that it has been an attempt "to defend the kind of poetry he is writing, or to formulate the kind he wants to write," and again, that "its merits and its limitations can be fully appreciated only when it is considered in relation to the poetry I have written myself."

Eliot's boyhood enthusiasms for poetry were commonplace enough, and yet they also prefigure his own development. At the age of fourteen he was deeply impressed and excited by the *Rubáiyát*, and then by Byron and Swinburne — for all the differences, a body of poetry marked by melancholy, cynicism, and cleverness. But it was at about the age of nineteen, while he was a junior at Harvard University, that an event took place which was to be of the greatest importance to Eliot as a poet — and to the course of English poetry in the twentieth century. The event was his discovery of *The Symbolist Movement in Literature,* a book on the French symbolist writers of the nineteenth century by the English critic Arthur Symons. Eliot was eventually to be influenced, in a general way, by several of the French poets, from Baudelaire to Mallarmé, but it was Jules Laforgue, discovered through Symons' book, who was to have by far the greatest effect. Eliot's acknowledgment of this is well known: "The form in which I began to write, in 1908 or 1909, was directly drawn from the study of Laforgue together with the later Elizabethan drama; and I do not know anyone who started from exactly that point." Insofar as Eliot started from an *exact point*, it was exclusively and emphatically the poetry of Laforgue. The later Elizabethan dramatists had a less immediate and less intense effect, and their influence is not positively apparent until "Gerontion," which was written about ten years after the initial encounter with Laforgue. The early poems published in the *Harvard Advocate* during 1909–10 read like translations or adaptations from Laforgue. "Conversation Galante," included in *Prufrock and Other Observations*, still has a highly imitative quality and serves very well to illustrate the first stages of influence. The poem is obviously modeled on "Autre Complainte de Lord Pierrot," which is quoted entire by Symons. These two stanzas are enough to show the closeness between the two poems:

> Et si ce cri lui part: "Dieu de Dieu que je t'aime!"
> — "Dieu reconnaîtra les siens." Ou piquée au vif:
> — "Mes claviers ont du cœur, tu sera mon seul thème."
> Moi: "Tout est relatif."

\*　　\*　　\*

> And I then: "Someone frames upon the keys
> That exquisite nocturne, with which we explain
> The night and moonshine; music which we seize
> To body forth our own vacuity."
>     She then: "Does this refer to me?"
> "Oh no, it is I who am inane."

If we consider these two poems, Laforgue's and Eliot's, and then recall Eliot's "Portrait of a Lady," it is easy to see how that poem, too, is another *conversation galante*, a dialogue between a man and a woman in which at once too much and too little is being communicated. In like manner, the *Harvard Advocate* poem called "Spleen" may be seen as a rudimentary form of "The Love Song of J. Alfred Prufrock." This early poem records the distraction and dejection produced by the "procession . . . of Sunday faces," by the social routines of the day and the sordid aspects of an urban alley, and then ends with a personification of "Life" as a balding and graying man, fastidiously attired and mannered, waiting with self-conscious correctness as a social caller upon the "Absolute." But "Prufrock" is also related to the "Portrait" and "Conversation Galante." The poem opens with the promise "To lead you to an overwhelming question . . ." and this question is not so much an interrogation as a problem — the problem of communication between a man and a woman.

> And would it have been worth it, after all,
> After the cups, the marmalade, the tea,
>
> .  .  .  .  .  .  .  .  .  .  .  .  .
>
> To have squeezed the universe into a ball
> To roll it toward some overwhelming question,
> To say: "I am Lazarus, come from the dead,
> Come back to tell you all, I shall tell you all" —
> If one, settling a pillow by her head
>     Should say: "That is not what I meant at all.
>     That is not it, at all."

This theme of the failure of communication, of a positive relationship, between a man and a woman is found again in the other early poems "Hysteria" and "La Figlia che Piange," and it is indeed a major theme of the whole body of Eliot's work. It appears early in *The Waste Land* with the image of the "hyacinth girl."

—Yet when we came back, late, from the Hyacinth garden,
Your arms full, and your hair wet, I could not
Speak, and my eyes failed, I was neither
Living nor dead, and I knew nothing,
Looking into the heart of light, the silence.

This theme is developed by various means throughout Eliot's poetry and plays. It becomes related to other emerging themes, especially to religious meanings — for example, in the symbolic imagery of the "rose-garden" which appears in the works *Ash Wednesday, Four Quartets, The Family Reunion*, and *The Confidential Clerk*.

## II

One of the most familiar aspects of Eliot's poetry is its complex echoing of multiple sources. In the early poems, those of the "Prufrock" period, this aspect is not yet very marked, but it is nonetheless already present in some degree. The title "Portrait of a Lady" immediately suggests Henry James, and there is indeed much about this poetry which is Jamesian. For one thing, the theme of the man-woman relationship frustrated or imperfectly realized is a common one in James's fiction. Commentators have noticed particularly a similarity of situations in Eliot's poem and the short novel called *The Beast in the Jungle* — in which the protagonist becomes poignantly and devastatingly aware of a woman's love for him only after she has died. Besides this specific similarity, there is a general Jamesian atmosphere which pervades the early poems. The man and woman of the "Portrait," Prufrock himself, "The readers of the *Boston Evening Transcript*," Aunt Helen, Cousin Nancy, the foreign Mr. Apollinax and his American hosts, all are Jamesian personae. Eliot, like James, presents a world of genteel society, as it is seen from within, but seen also with critical penetration, with a consciousness that is deliberately and intensely self-consciousness. Both writers, in their ultimate meanings, show a liberation from the genteel standard of decorum, while the style and manner which have familiarly attended the decorum not only remain, but have become more complicated and

intense. After the period of the early poems, the Jamesian qualities, like the Laforguean, are not abandoned but are assimilated
and survive in the later stages of development. The opening
strophe of *The Waste Land*, with its vision of a cosmopolitan society, ends on a Jamesian note: "I read, much of the night, and
go south in the winter." The Jamesian quality emerges with great
clarity in all the plays on contemporary subjects. They are all set
in James-like genteel worlds. Such dramatic intensity as they have
resides, as in so much of James's fiction, in crises of sensibility
and awareness. Significantly enough, a specific Jamesian note is
strongly sounded at the opening of the earliest of these plays. In
the very first minute of *The Family Reunion* Ivy echoes *The Waste
Land* with rather heavy emphasis:

> I have always told Amy she should go south in the winter.
> Were I in Amy's position, I would go south in the winter.
>
> · · · · · · · · · · · · · · · · · · · ·
>
> I would go south in the winter, if I could afford it . . .

In the same scene, only a few minutes later, Agatha is commenting
on Harry's return to his parental home, and she speaks the phrase
"it will not be a very *jolly* corner," thus invoking Henry James,
who had written a story called "The Jolly Corner," also about a
man's homecoming and his search for an earlier identity.

While the theme of estrangement between man and woman is,
so to speak, an ultimate subject throughout much of Eliot's work,
it also signifies the larger theme of the individual's isolation, his
estrangement from other people and from the world. There are
intimations of this larger theme even in "Portrait of a Lady,"
where the young man's twice-mentioned "self-possession" means
not only his poise but, in the Eliotic context, his isolation, his
inability to give himself to or to possess others. In "Prufrock" the
theme of isolation is pervasive and represented in various ways,
from the "patient etherised upon a table," at the beginning, to
the mermaids, at the end, who will not "sing to me" — but especially in the well-known lines

> I should have been a pair of ragged claws
> Scuttling across the floors of silent seas.

13

In a sense, all of Eliot's works in verse are variations on the theme of isolation. *The Waste Land* presents a procession of characters locked within themselves. The subject emerges into definition toward the end of the poem.

> We think of the key, each in his prison
> Thinking of the key, each confirms a prison . . .

When we turn to the plays, we find characters either accepting isolation or struggling to escape from it. In *Murder in the Cathedral*, the saint, Thomas, is by definition set apart from ordinary humanity. Harry, toward the end of *The Family Reunion*, says, "Where does one go from a world of insanity?" — and the implication of his subsequent and final statement is that he goes the way of the saint and the martyr. This is the way, too, that Celia Coplestone goes in *The Cocktail Party*, while the estranged Edward and Lavinia Chamberlayne are reconciled, not to love, or even to understanding, but merely to mutual toleration, making "the best of a bad job." The theme of isolation is in focus throughout the play, and with especial clarity in such words as these of Celia to the psychiatrist, Sir Henry Harcourt-Reilly:

> No . . . it isn't that I *want* to be alone,
> But that everyone's alone — or so it seems to me.
> They make noises, and think that they are talking
>     to each other;
> They make faces, and think they understand each other.
> And I'm sure that they don't.

Unlike the earlier plays, *The Confidential Clerk* contains no suggestion of the martyred saint, but nonetheless the central character, Colby Simpkins, like Harry and Celia before him, goes his own way. Finally indifferent as to who are his earthly parents, he turns to religion, first to be a church organist, and probably in time an Anglican clergyman. *The Cocktail Party* and *The Confidential Clerk* are each in turn, and with increasing measure, departures from the extreme and intense isolation represented in *The Family Reunion*. In *The Cocktail Party* marriage is regarded as a way of life, though cheerless, yet necessary and acceptable, "the common routine." *The Confidential Clerk* offers a brighter perspective on marriage and on the possibilities of mutual sympathy and understanding among human beings.

Then, with *The Elder Statesman*, there is the most marked departure of all from the theme of isolation. Lord Claverton, invalided and retired statesman and business executive of hollow success, has been a failure as friend, lover, husband, and father. His frustrations and anxieties are dramatized by the return of the man and woman whom in his youth he had abused. But his daughter Monica and her fiancé Charles encourage him to explain his problems, and in explaining he confesses all the pretenses and deceptions of his life, while they listen with an understanding and sympathy which restore him to himself and thus release him from his isolation. He discovers not only the love which Monica and Charles have for him, but also the love which they have for each other. In *The Elder Statesman*, Eliot has for the first time depicted with ardency and exaltation real and normal relations between a man and a woman. Toward the very end of the play, Charles tells Monica that he loves her "to the limits of speech, and beyond." And she replies that she has loved him "from the beginning of the world," that this love which has brought them together "was always there," before either of them was born. As compared with Eliot's other plays, there is no apparent religious dimension in *The Elder Statesman* — except for the intimations of these words of Monica. The play as a whole is an affirmation of human relations, a drama of escape from isolation within the limits of those relations.

It has been said of some writers that they write as if no one has ever written before. Of Eliot it is the reverse which is true — and true with a special significance, so that one cannot speak of his *sources* in the usual scholarly fashion. The point is that Eliot has been in a respect his own scholar, having brought to his work not only the influence of his sources but what might more aptly be called an awareness of his predecessors. This is true in a variety of ways. For example, the theme of isolation is so obviously universal and so readily available that a writer might very well pursue it without any awareness of particular antecedents or analogues. But for Eliot there is such an awareness. This is indicated by the foot-note which Eliot fixed to the "key-prison" passage of *The Waste Land.* The footnote refers us to *Appearance and Reality*, a work by the British philosopher F. H. Bradley, and quotes as follows from that work: "My external sensations are no less private to myself than are my thoughts or my feelings. In either case my ex-perience falls within my own circle, a circle closed on the outside; and, with all its elements alike, every sphere is opaque to the others which surround it. . . . In brief, regarded as an existence which appears in a soul, the whole world for each is peculiar and private to that soul." Eliot's deep interest in this idealist philosopher is indicated by his Harvard doctoral thesis (1916), "Experience and the Objects of Knowledge in the Philosophy of F. H. Bradley," and by a few other pieces, one of which is included in his *Selected Essays.* The Bradleyan element in Eliot's thought emerges as an echo of the circle image in one of the choruses of *The Family Reunion.*

> But the circle of our understanding
> Is a very restricted area.
> Except for a limited number
> Of strictly practical purposes
> We do not know what we are doing;
> And even, when you think of it,
> We do not know much about thinking.
> What is happening outside of the circle?
> And what is the meaning of happening?

Eliot has defined his position by vividly portraying the world from which he is isolated and alienated. This practice is consistent with the Bradleyan philosophy. The individual mood, the quality of consciousness, the private feeling, is continuous with, in a sense identical with, the seemingly objective material that has provoked it. A person's identity is defined by his world, and to escape one is as difficult as to escape the other. This concept is implied in that early poem "Spleen," where a "waste land" is already beginning to emerge, where an environment of people and things is a "dull conspiracy" against which depression is "unable to rally." Pru-frock's escape to the beautiful and the ideal from the ugly and the real, his reverie of the mermaids, is only momentarily sustained, "Till human voices wake us, and we drown."

Characteristically, the moments of beauty in Eliot's work are meager and brief and are obviously calculated to serve as a contrasting emphasis on the opposite, as in *The Waste Land*:

> . . . the nightingale
> Filled all the desert with inviolable voice
> And still she cried, and still the world pursues,
> "Jug Jug" to dirty ears.

Up through *The Waste Land* Eliot's poetry is richly furnished with images of the sordid, the disgusting, and the depressing, and with personalities of similar quality. In the poems of the "Prufrock" group (1917) there are the one-night cheap hotels and sawdust restaurants, the vacant lots, faint stale smells of beer, a thousand furnished rooms and the yellow soles of feet, the dead geraniums, the broken spring in a factory yard, all the old nocturnal smells, the basement kitchens, and the damp souls of housemaids. In the poems of the "Gerontion" group (1920), there are "Rocks, moss, stonecrop, iron, merds," and such obnoxious persons as Bleistein, Sweeney, and Grishkin. *The Waste Land* (1922) and *The Hollow Men* (1925) are titles indicating clearly enough the grounds of alienation. *The Waste Land* is a grand consummation of the themes, techniques, and styles that Eliot had been developing, and *The Hollow Men* is at once an epilogue to that development and a prologue to a new stage in the career.

The new stage is marked by the difference between the titles *The Hollow Men* and *Ash Wednesday* (1930), and by Eliot's entry into the Church of England in 1927. But the new stage is not, of course, a sudden and abrupt change. Its emergence may be seen, especially in retrospect, in the prose — even as early as 1917, the date of "Tradition and the Individual Talent," which is relevant both by its title and its general argument — and the emergence may be seen in the poetry as well. The continuity of Eliot's poetry is, indeed, most impressive, already indicated here in some measure, and will be further considered. For the moment, it is appropriate to observe that *The Waste Land* and *The Hollow Men* have in retrospect been considered more Christian than they originally appeared to be. The way in which theme and imagery of *The Waste Land* blend and merge into those of *Ash Wednesday* is illustrated by these passages from *The Hollow Men*:

> This is the dead land
> This is cactus land
> Here the stone images
> Are raised, here they receive
> The supplication of a dead man's hand
> Under the twinkle of a fading star.

> \*     \*     \*

> Sightless, unless
> The eyes reappear
> As the perpetual star
> Multifoliate rose
> Of death's twilight kingdom
> The hope only
> Of empty men.

The rocks that are red in *The Waste Land* reappear in *Ash Wednesday* as cool and blue. In the one poem there is the lament "Amongst the rocks one cannot stop or think," while the other poem moves toward conclusion with the prayer

> Teach us to care and not to care
> Teach us to sit still
> Even among these rocks.

Eliot's deliberate echoing of the earlier poem in the later one signifies that the difference in position is produced by a development rather than a departure or a break. While the position of isolation and alienation from the world is the foremost theme of the poetry up through *The Waste Land*, the same position, but with respect to God, is the theme of *Ash Wednesday*. Thus the first position, considered as a problem, has not been resolved. It has, rather, been incorporated into the second position and thus reinterpreted and re-evaluated. If one does not love the world, one is already well prepared for making an effort to love God. Isolation and alienation from the world become a stage in the discipline of religious purgation, an ideal to be further pursued. With Eliot's profession of Christian belief, this is the meaning which has been found in the lines concluding *The Waste Land*:

> Shall I at least set my lands in order?
> London Bridge is falling down falling down
>    falling down
> *Poi s'ascose nel foco che gli affina* . . .

### III

The idea of isolation, of the impossibility of communication and understanding, has a direct bearing on Eliot's style, his mode of composition, and the structure of his poems, for the thematic problem is not only that of communication between one person and another but, finally, that of articulation itself. Prufrock, toward the end of his monologue, declares,

> It is impossible to say just what I mean!
> But as if a magic lantern threw the nerves in
>    patterns on a screen . . .

This statement has a multiplicity of implications which are appropriate to Eliot's work, both the poetry and the criticism. The statement is Prufrock's, and it is also Eliot's, spoken through the mask of Prufrock. We may consider first its relevance to the poem in which it occurs. A familiar complaint about Eliot's early poetry, including "Prufrock," was that it was difficult, obscure, and so on — that it did not clearly and directly say what it means. And indeed, it does not. Instead, like the magic lantern, it throws "the nerves in patterns on a screen." The poem "Prufrock" is like a series of slides. Each slide is an isolated, fragmentary image, producing its own effect, including suggestions of some larger action or situation of which it is but an arrested moment. For example, "Prufrock" proceeds from the half-deserted streets at evening, to the women coming and going, to the yellow fog, to Prufrock descending the stair, and so on, to the mermaids at the end of the poem. Each part of the poem, each fragment, remains fragmentary even within its given context — a series of larger wholes is suggested, and yet the series of suggestions is itself a kind of whole. It is the poem. It is Prufrock. He has gone nowhere and done nothing. He has conducted an "interior monologue," as the critics have said, and he is the monologue. All the scenery of the poem, indoor and outdoor, is finally the psychological landscape of Prufrock himself. The streets, rooms, people, and fancies of the poem all register on Prufrock's consciousness, and thus they are his consciousness, the man himself. Prufrock the man, his self-awareness, his state of feeling — each is equal to the other, and to his *meaning*. In order to say *just what* he means, he must render the essential man himself, he must throw, as it were ("But as if"), the nerves in patterns on a screen. But so to project the *real* nerves, the feelings in all their fullness which are the man himself, is impossible. It is the incommunicable secret of the mystics, and the ideal of romantic lovers. It is also the myth of romantic poets, from Byron and Shelley to Whitman, and since then. And it is distinctive of Eliot's modernness, of his modern romanticism, that he knows that it is a myth, while still recognizing the impulse (which is not the same as the desire) to pursue it.

Emerging from these considerations of "Prufrock" are generalizations which are applicable to all of Eliot's poetry. The characteristic poem, whether "Prufrock" or other, is analogous to the series of slides, highly selective and suggestive. And like "Prufrock," the poem contains a statement acknowledging this aspect of the poem and of its structure. (In this regard Eliot is more conservative than the French symbolist poets who served him as model and authority for this mode of composition.) "Preludes" is a series of four sketches of urban scenes in winter, followed by an explicatory comment:

> I am moved by fancies that are curled
> Around these images, and cling:
> The notion of some infinitely gentle
> Infinitely suffering thing.

"These images" constitute the main body of the poem. The poet has tried to guide the reader toward the "meaning" of the poem by mentioning the "fancies" which attend the images, and then by illustrating with a particular "notion." There are still other fancies or notions in the conclusion to the poem.

> Wipe your hands across your mouth, and laugh;
> The worlds revolve like ancient women
> Gathering fuel in vacant lots.

The final image picks up thematically from the first scene the image of "newspapers from vacant lots." The poem thus ends on the note of the fragmentary, which is in various senses the subject of the poem.

In the earlier stages of Eliot's development "Prufrock," "Gerontion," and *The Waste Land* are obviously the major landmarks. Each of these poems in turn deepens, expands, and complicates features of the preceding poem, and among such features are the theme of alienation, the fragmentary quality of the parts, and finally the acknowledgment of these within the poem. While Prufrock exclaims that it is impossible to say just what he means, Gerontion announces that he has lost all the faculties of perception:

> I have lost my sight, smell, hearing, taste and touch:
> How should I use them for your closer contact?

And Gerontion concludes with a statement which is a characterization of the monologue he has delivered:

> Tenants of the house,
> Thoughts of a dry brain in a dry season.

At the opening of the poem he calls himself "A dull head among windy spaces," and thus at the opening and close of the poem there are justifications, and hence admissions, of the nature of the poem — of its lack of conventional continuity and coherence. It is the critics who have described "Prufrock" as an "interior monologue," but it was Eliot himself who indicated the peculiarly private relevance of "Gerontion": "Thoughts of a dry brain."

As for *The Waste Land*, only a few reminders serve well to evoke the central themes and general qualities of that work. "A heap of broken images"; "I could not/ Speak"; "Is there nothing in your head?"; "I can connect/ Nothing with nothing"; "We think of the key, each in his prison." And then finally, at the end of the poem, among the collection of quoted fragments, there is the statement "These fragments I have shored against my ruins."

The fragments are, of course, the amalgam of quotations in which the statement is imbedded. But the statement may also be taken as a reference to the entire poem, for the whole of *The Waste Land* is in a respect an amalgam of quotations, of fragments. At the opening there are the snatches of conversation, and then the poem is under way, with the addition of fragment to fragment, selected parts of a variety of sources mingled together and flowing into each other, the sources being life itself past and present as well as writings, until all the broken images are assembled into the heap which is the poem itself, the completed mixture of memory and desire. The series of fragments at the end compresses and intensifies the technique, the mode of expression, which has operated throughout the poem. In this respect, the very technique of the poem, especially as symbolized by the conclusion, is significant of the poet's meaning — or of part of his meaning — which is his despair of ever succeeding in fully articulating his meaning. If the poet's own voice finally fails him, he can at least intimate that much, confirm his prison, by withdrawing almost altogether, while the poem dies away with the echo of other voices, and thus reaches a termination which is, appropriately, not altogether a conclusion. It is impossible for the poet to say *just* what he means, and yet he manages to say that much. And to say that much, to say it effectively, to make the claim persuasively, is after all a kind of consummation. If he could have entirely articulated his meaning, then it would no longer have been the meaning with which he was concerned.

There are external facts related to these subjects of the fragmentary and the problem of articulation. It is well known, for example, that the form in which *The Waste Land* was published was the result of Ezra Pound's extensive editing of Eliot's manuscript. We do not know precisely and fully what changes Pound made, for the original manuscript seems to be irretrievably lost. But we know quite a bit, from surviving correspondence between Pound and Eliot and from Eliot's testimony. Pound persuaded Eliot not to use as epigraph a quotation from Conrad's *Heart of Darkness*, not to use "Gerontion" as a prelude to *The Waste Land*, to retain the section called "Death by Water" (which is Eliot's translation of his own French verses in "Dans le Restaurant"), and to accept excisions which reduced the poem to about half its original length. Eliot's decision to accept Pound's recommendations is, of course, part of his own creative responsibility and achievement, but it also forcibly illustrates the essential fragmentariness of Eliot's work. *The Waste Land* could survive, and with benefit, the amputation of fragments because it was and is essentially an arrangement of fragments. But it is no more so than the poetry that had been written earlier and the poetry that was to follow. Both *The Hollow Men* and *Ash Wednesday* began as short individual poems published independently in periodicals, and the pieces were later fitted together and other sections added to make the completed longer poems. This piecemeal mode of composition is emphasized by the fact that some of the short poems written during the same period and having similar themes, style, and imagery are excluded from *The Hollow Men* and in the collected editions preserved among the "Minor Poems." There is a nice implication here — that "minor" pieces, when assembled under an inclusive title and according to some thematic and cumulative principle, produce a "major" and more formidable whole. The relationship between whole and parts is again suggested by the "Ariel Poems," first published between 1927 and 1930 (except for "The Cultivation of Christmas Trees," 1954), the same period during which *Ash Wednesday* was taking shape. The earlier "Ariel Poems" are closely related in structure, style, and meaning to those poems which eventually became sections of *Ash Wednesday*. It is conceivable that some of the "Ariel Poems" might have been built into larger wholes and the earliest sections of *Ash Wednesday* left as separate poems. As it is, the "Ariel Poems" make a kind of series of appendixes to *Ash Wednesday*.

Turning from the external to the internal, we find in *The Hollow Men* and *Ash Wednesday* the same features already noted in earlier work. In *The Hollow Men* the themes of the fragmentary and the inarticulate are represented by both the form and the content of the statements. Throughout the poem the themes are symbolized by a wealth of images, and especially notable are "broken glass," "broken column," "broken stone," and "broken jaw." At the opening of the poem the voices of the hollow men "Are quiet and meaningless," and toward the end their speech is broken into stammered fragments of the Lord's Prayer. The first and last passages of the final section are inane and sinister parodies of a children's game song. Similar elements are present in *Ash Wednesday*. The poem begins with the translated quotation from Cavalcanti, and this is immediately broken into fragments, thus suggesting, among other things, the speaker's struggle to find expression:

> Because I do not hope to turn again
> Because I do not hope
> Because I do not hope to turn . . .

Exactly the same passage, but with "Because" changed to "Although," opens the final section of the poem. Section II is centrally concerned with fragmentation as symbolized by the scattered bones which sing, "We are glad to be scattered, we did little good to each other." As for the problem of articulation, it is the "unspoken word" which is the central concern of section V:

> Where shall the word be found, where will the word
> Resound? Not here, there is not enough silence
> Not on the sea or on the islands, not
> On the mainland, in the desert or the rain land . . .

The final words of the poem are "Suffer me not to be separated/ And let my cry come unto Thee." These statements are fragments quoted from Catholic ritual — and they clearly convey both of the familiar and related themes: isolation (which is also fragmentation) and spiritual communion (which is also articulation).

In the collected editions of Eliot's poetry, placed between "Ariel Poems" and "Minor Poems," there is a section called "Unfinished Poems." This is comprised of *Sweeney Agonistes* and "Coriolan." The two parts of *Sweeney Agonistes* are "Fragment of a Prologue" and "Fragment of an Agon," and they first appeared in 1926 and 1927 respectively. Arranged together, they are described by Eliot in a subtitle as "Fragments of an Aristophanic Melodrama." But *Sweeney Agonistes* is not actually an "unfinished" work. Each part and the two parts together are deliberate ironical parodies of surviving fragments of classical texts, and thus the fragmentariness is a justifiable aspect of the finished product. The device of parodying (classical) fragments provided Eliot with an opportunity for experimental exercises in the use of dramatic verse and thus also in the use of rhythms borrowed from the conventions of the music hall and of colloquial speech. Another aspect of the fragmentariness is the deliberate continuity with, or reiteration of, elements from his earlier work — meaning, of course, that Sweeney had first appeared in the quatrains of *Poems* (1920) and then again briefly in *The Waste Land*. In the satirically trite and empty speech which makes up so much of the dialogue in these pieces, the subject of articulation, of communication, is plainly implicit, and it is finally explicit in the lines spoken by Sweeney toward the end of the second "Fragment":

> I gotta use words when I talk to you
> But if you understand or if you dont
> That's nothing to me and nothing to you . . .

The fragmentariness of *Sweeney Agonistes* is a structural device, but also, as in earlier works, it is related to subject and meaning. "Coriolan," on the other hand, is appropriately described as "unfinished." Its two sections, "Triumphal March" and "Difficulties of a Statesman," appeared respectively in 1931 and 1932. The work was apparently motivated by the political pressures of the time. Eliot's description of "Coriolan" as unfinished is meaningful in a number of ways. It obviously signifies that a suite of sections constituting a larger and self-contained work was intended. Eliot clearly abandoned the project at an early date, for in *Collected Poems 1909–1935* the work is already classified as unfinished. And "Coriolan" does have a quality of incompleteness in greater measure than is characteristic of Eliot's work. There is, for example, more "completeness," more clarity of effect, a more decided achievement of tone, in any section of *The Waste Land* or *The Hollow Men* or *Ash Wednesday*. Perhaps Eliot was aware of this measure of failure in deciding to abandon the project and then to classify it as unfinished. It was, in fact, uncharacteristic of Eliot to have projected a poem on so large a scale, and the failure of the project is therefore significant. When questioned by an interviewer, Eliot clearly acknowledged what was otherwise implicit in his practice. To the question whether *Ash Wednesday* had begun as separate poems, he answered: "Yes, like *The Hollow Men*, it originated out of separate poems. . . . Then gradually I came to see it as a sequence. That's one way in which my mind does seem to have worked throughout the years poetically — doing things separately and then seeing the possibility of fusing them together, altering them, and making a kind of whole of them."

A *kind* of whole — that is an apt and significant description. That kind of whole is nowhere more obvious than in what appears to be Eliot's final major performance in nondramatic verse, the *Four Quartets*. He has informed us that the first of these, *Burnt Norton*, grew out of passages deleted from his play *Murder in the Cathedral*. The *Four Quartets* was hardly conceived as "a kind of whole" at the time of the composition of *Burnt Norton*. That poem, eventually to be the first Quartet, appeared in 1935, and the next Quartet, *East Coker*, not until 1940. Thus the *Four Quartets* had an unpremeditated beginning in the salvaging of fragments removed from the play. *Burnt Norton* itself becomes a "kind of fragment" in retrospect from the other Quartets. In the years immediately following its appearance it received relatively little attention, while the *Four Quartets* was soon, and then often, praised as Eliot's supreme achievement. By itself, *Burnt Norton* revealed themes and elements of structure familiar enough against the background of earlier work. Like *The Waste Land*, it is divided into five sections. It has affinities of meaning and style with *Ash Wednesday* and *Murder in the Cathedral*, and also with the play *The Family Reunion*, which came later (1939). But in serving as the model for the other three quartets, it derived a clarity of structure and patterning of themes which could not otherwise be claimed for it. To extend the musical metaphor of the inclusive title, it is the variations which locate and define the theme. And it is that title which announces most succinctly the quasi-wholeness and the quasi-fragmentariness which are characteristic of Eliot's work. The title *Four Quartets* allows for the separate unity of each of the Quartets, and at the same time makes each a part of the larger whole.

While this ambivalence of parts and wholes is a structural convenience of which Eliot had always availed himself, it operates with special purpose in *Four Quartets*. A central subject of the work is the relation of the individual consciousness and identity to the passage of time — and time is meaningful in the work not only as a consideration and a grounds of discourse, but also in respect to the history of the composition of *Four Quartets*, to its having been written over a period of time. During this period of time there were changes in the poet's attitudes. According to *Burnt Norton*, "To be conscious is not to be in time." Escape from time into consciousness is achieved in the transcendent ecstasy symbolized by "the moment in the rose-garden," so that all other time, unless it is a means to this end, is meaningless:

> Ridiculous the waste sad time
> Stretching before and after.

The later Quartets, on the other hand, are less subjective and are increasingly concerned with reconciling the temporal and the timeless — as toward the end of *The Dry Salvages*:

> . . . And right action is freedom
> From past and future also.
> For most of us, this is the aim
> Never here to be realised;
> Who are only undefeated
> Because we have gone on trying . . .

*Four Quartets* is (or are) essentially meditative and reflective poetry, but the mode of composition over a period of time, the fresh attack in each Quartet on the same themes, the willingness to acknowledge and define changes in attitude — these give a dramatic quality to the reflections. The changes wrought by time are thus not only a general subject of the work, they are a particularized and dramatized meaning, and in being such they are also a lineament of the form. The poet's awareness of this fact is among the reflections he makes in the poetry. In *East Coker* there is the plaintive observation that "every attempt/ Is a wholly new start," and in *The Dry Salvages* the problem is expressed again, this time as a broader, less subjectively personal preoccupation:

> . . . time is no healer: the patient is no longer here.
>
> · · · · · · · · · · · · · · · ·
>
> You are not the same people who left that station
> Or who will arrive at any terminus . . .

Each of the Quartets and then all of them together have a greater conventional unity than Eliot's previous nondramatic poetry. Whereas so much of the earlier work is a direct representation of the fragmentariness of experience, *Four Quartets* is a deliberate and sustained discourse on that subject, and it ends with a serene vision of that wholeness which lies beyond the reach of time:

> And all shall be well and
> All manner of thing shall be well
> When the tongues of flame are in-folded
> Into the crowned knot of fire
> And the fire and the rose are one.

As in earlier work, the problem of articulation is among the interrelated themes of *Four Quartets*. In *Ash Wednesday* blame was placed upon the external world for this problem:

> . . . there is not enough silence
>
> · · · · · · · · · · ·
>
> The right time and the right place are not here . . .

The same complaint is made in the early Quartets, as in the final section of *Burnt Norton*:

> . . . Words strain,
> Crack and sometimes break, under the burden,
> Under the tension, slip, slide, perish,
> Decay with imprecision, will not stay in place,
> Will not stay still. Shrieking voices
> Scolding, mocking, or merely chattering,
> Always assail them.

In *East Coker* the poet complains of "the intolerable wrestle/ With words and meanings." If it is impossible to say just what he means, this is because his meanings have changed with the passage of time,

Because one has only learnt to get the better of words
For the thing one no longer has to say, or the
    way in which
One is no longer disposed to say it.

Blame is still put upon the external world, for the struggle must be made, he says,

            . . . now, under conditions
        That seem unpropitious.

In the final Quartet, *Little Gidding*, there is greater candor, greater objectivity, an acknowledgment of his own achievement, but still a note of alienation, as the poet sees his work (so long a dominant and determining influence) recede with the passage of time into the perspective of literary history:

        . . . Last season's fruit is eaten
    And the fullfed beast shall kick the empty pail.
        For last year's words belong to last year's language
        And next year's words await another voice.

In the last section of *Little Gidding* there is a final statement on the subject, a statement which combines a celebration of the possible with an acceptance of the inevitable.

        . . . And every phrase
        And sentence that is right (where every word is
            at home,
        Taking its place to support the others,
        The word neither diffident nor ostentatious,
        An easy commerce of the old and the new,
        The common word exact without vulgarity,
        The formal word precise but not pedantic,
        The complete consort dancing together)
        Every phrase and every sentence is an end and
            a beginning,
        Every poem an epitaph.

As already noted, the isolation of the individual is a theme of Eliot's plays, and closely related to it is the problem of articulation and mutual understanding. In *The Cocktail Party*, two ways of life are set in contrast, the way of the saint and the way of ordinary experience. While it is allowed that "Both ways are necessary," that a choice must be made of one or the other, and that the ordinary way is not inferior, it is nonetheless presented unattractively. Husband and wife, representing the ordinary way, are described as

> Two people who know they do not understand each other,
> Breeding children whom they do not understand
> And who will never understand them.

If in *The Cocktail Party* there is an affirmation of the ordinary way, this affirmation includes the attitude of being resigned to isolation. With *The Confidential Clerk*, however, the polarities of absolute isolation and absolute understanding are resolved by the acceptance of intermediate possibilities, of partial understanding. Colby Simpkins, the young confidential clerk, speaks of the limitations of mutual understanding not as a negative aspect of human relations but as a ground for mutual respect:

> I meant, there's no end to understanding a person.
> All one can do is to understand them better,
> To keep up with them; so that as the other changes
> You can understand the change as soon as it happens,
> Though you couldn't have predicted it.

*The Confidential Clerk* ends on the theme of understanding between husband and wife and between parents and children. The aging couple, Sir Claude and Lady Elizabeth, have finally achieved a measure of understanding with each other. When she says, "Claude, we've got to try to understand our children," her illegitimate son (who is engaged to his illegitimate daughter) says, "And we should like to understand *you*." *The Elder Statesman* similarly finds dramatic resolution in the understanding achieved between the generations, between the father on the one hand and the daughter and her fiancé on the other. Toward the end of the play the familiar problem of articulation arises between the lovers, when Charles tells Monica that he loves her beyond "the limits of speech," and that the lover, despite the inadequacy of words, must still struggle for them as the asthmatic struggles for breath. Not the measure of communication achieved, but the will and effort to communicate receive the emphasis here.

In the dedicatory verses to his wife at the opening of the published volume of *The Elder Statesman*, Eliot returns yet again to the matter of words and meanings. In this poem he speaks of himself and his wife as "lovers" who share each other's thoughts "without need of speech" and who "babble . . . without need of meaning." The dedication ends with the statement that some of the words of the play have a special meaning "For you and me only." These lines document the extreme change in attitude that has taken place since Eliot first recorded Prufrock's lament that he could linger among the sea-girls of his restrained erotic fantasies only "Till human voices wake us, and we drown." In these lines to his wife he celebrates a mutual understanding which requires no articulation and a speech which does not strain toward meaning. In the final lines there is again the matter of words and meanings, and of isolation, but it is an isolation which is shared — "For you and me only" — and thus it is also communion — but still, in a sense, isolation. Hence, Eliot has changed his attitude without departing from his theme. "A Dedication to My Wife," with some interesting revisions, is included in *Collected Poems 1909–1962*.

## IV

In his criticism Eliot has said a number of times that the entire output of certain writers constitutes a single work, that there is a meaningful interrelationship of compositions, and that individual pieces are endowed with meaning by other pieces and by the whole context of a writer's work. Like so many of Eliot's generalizations, this is particularly applicable to his own poetry. If there is a fragmentary aspect to much of his work, there is also a continuity and wholeness. As we have already seen, a frequent practice of Eliot's was "doing things separately" and then "making a kind of whole of them," so that the fragmentary quality of the work is finally operative in the unity of the whole. The recurrent themes of time, alienation, isolation, and articulation obviously contribute to the continuity. And so does a steadily developing pattern of interrelated images, symbols, and themes. There is for example, the underwater imagery of the poems of the "Prufrock" group:

I should have been a pair of ragged claws
Scuttling across the floors of silent seas.

\* \* \*

We have lingered in the chambers of the sea
By sea-girls wreathed with seaweed red and brown
Till human voices wake us, and we drown.

\* \* \*

The memory throws up high and dry
A crowd of twisted things;
A twisted branch upon the beach . . .

\* \* \*

The brown waves of fog toss up to me
Twisted faces from the bottom of the street . . .

\* \* \*

His laughter was submarine and profound
Like the old man of the sea's
Hidden under coral islands
Where worried bodies of drowned men drift
    down in the green silence,
Dropping from fingers of surf.

Comparable images, of water and underwater, of rain and river and sea, continue to appear throughout the poetry, reflecting and echoing each other with cumulative effect. There is a similar development of flower and garden imagery, from beginning to end, and extending into the plays. The "hyacinth girl" of *The Waste Land* is related to the "smell of hyacinths" in "Portrait of a Lady," to the girl, "her arms full of flowers," in "La Figlia che Piange," and to the little girl ("Elle était toute mouillée, je lui ai donné des primevères") of "Dans le Restaurant." The rose-garden dialogue of Harry and Agatha in *The Family Reunion* remains enigmatic unless related to this garden imagery in Eliot's poetry, and especially to the symbolic rose-gardens of *Ash Wednesday* and *Burnt Norton*. Each garden passage, whether early or late, gains in clarity and scope of meaning when in relation to the others. At the outset of *The Confidential Clerk*, when Eggerson speaks of Colby —

He's expressed such an interest in my garden

That I think he ought to have window boxes.
Some day he'll want a garden of his own.

— the informed reader is alerted to the spiritual and religious intimations of the ecstatic childhood experience in the rose-garden,
variously represented elsewhere in Eliot's poetry. In addition to
such meaningful recurrence of symbolic imagery, there is at times
a merging of one kind of imagery with another, as in these lines
from "Marina":

Whispers and small laughter between leaves and hurrying feet
Under sleep, where all the waters meet.

Here the garden imagery and the water imagery are related to
each other, and related also to that deeper realm of consciousness
in which such associations occur. Two patterns of imagery, each
already intricate and extensive, have been joined to produce a
pattern that is still larger and more intricate.

In the continuity of Eliot's poetry, there is not only an accumulation of meaning but an alteration of meaning, a retroactive effect
of later elements upon earlier. For example, the lines quoted from
"Marina" have a relevance to the final lines of "Prufrock." Marina
is the girl, the daughter, in Shakespeare's *Pericles*, and, as her
name indicates, a "sea-girl." There are, thus, in both passages the
details of underwater, of sleep, and of the sea-girls. Considered
alone, the sexual fantasy of the earlier passage is expressive of
Prufrock's isolation and alienation — "Till human voices wake us,
and we drown." But when considered in relation to "Marina" and
to the entire pattern of the rose-garden imagery, Prufrock's erotic
daydream becomes an intimation of what is represented in later
poems as spiritual vision. The mermaids of Prufrock's self-indul-
gent reverie are an antecedent type of the female figure who is
later to represent spiritual guidance — such as the "Lady" in *Ash
Wednesday*, who is "spirit of the fountain, spirit of the garden
. . . spirit of the river, spirit of the sea."

Another example of retroactive effect is Eliot's use of ideas
found in the mystical work of St. John of the Cross, *The Dark
Night of the Soul*. The Spanish mystic outlines a course of spiritual discipline leading to purgation and spiritual rebirth. The

initial condition requisite for entering this discipline is described by St. John as of a negative nature, a state of inertia of sense and of spirit, the purpose being ultimately to eliminate the sensual and to bring the spiritual under control. This condition is one of isolation, alienation, bleakness, emptiness, dryness. St. John's system is summarized in *Burnt Norton* and *East Coker*, in each case in the final passage of section III — with particular clarity in *Burnt Norton*:

> Internal darkness, deprivation
> And destitution of all property,
> Desiccation of the world of sense,
> Evacuation of the world of fancy,
> Inoperancy of the world of spirit . . .

It is this system of spiritual discipline which provides the underlying scheme of *Ash Wednesday* and which is the clue to the meaning of that poem. The renunciation and impotency of section I, the dry and scattered bones of section II, seem to be a reiteration of the bleaker themes of *The Waste Land* and *The Hollow Men* — but with a difference. In *Ash Wednesday* there is an acceptance of the plight, and the bones sing, "We are glad to be scattered." The wasted and hollow condition, unrelieved in the earlier poems, is in *Ash Wednesday* a preparation for "strength beyond hope and despair" (section III). Hence the ambiguous prayer, in the first and last sections, "Teach us to care and not to care." In *Ash Wednesday* Eliot maintains the themes of the earlier poetry, but in relating them to St. John's system of spiritual discipline, the themes are reinterpreted and re-evaluated. Thus, from the perspective of *Ash Wednesday* and the *Four Quartets*, the earlier poetry takes on a meaning which it did not previously have. Once we have followed Eliot in relating his themes to St. John's system, the relevance extends to all expressions of the theme. The statement in "Gerontion," "I have lost my sight, smell, hearing, taste and touch," becomes an anticipation of "Desiccation of the world of sense." This is not to say that the earlier apparent meanings of "Gerontion," *The Waste Land*, and *The Hollow Men* are canceled out by the later poems, any more than one Quartet cancels another, or the later plays the earlier plays and poems. While each work remains itself, it takes on an additional aspect, a qualification of meaning, in the larger context. Eliot's observation, in "Tradition and the Individual Talent," about literature in general, that "the past [is] altered by the present as much as the present is directed by the past," is precisely applicable to his own career as a poet.

In discussing Eliot's poetry, we have, inevitably, considered some of the ways in which the poetry and the criticism are related to each other. This intricate and extensive subject has received the attention of numerous critics, including Eliot himself in recent years. But a few more illustrations of the relation will be appropriate and will serve as a further documentation of the emphases here pursued. It is particularly some of the more famous essays which lend themselves to this purpose. For example, in "The Metaphysical Poets" (1921) we find ideas which are applicable to Eliot's poetry, such as the following familiar passage: "We can only say that it appears likely that poets in our civilization, as it exists at present, must be *difficult*. Our civilization comprehends great variety and complexity, and this variety and complexity, playing upon a refined sensibility, must produce various and complex results. The poet must become more and more comprehensive, more allusive, more indirect, in order to force, to dislocate if necessary, language into his meaning." This belongs to the period of *The Waste Land*, and it is clearly enough an argument for such poetry. At the same time, one may see in this argument a recurring theme of Eliot's verse: the poet's struggle to state his meaning and the obstacles he faces in the contemporary world. Eliot offers the metaphysical poets as a precedent for this forcing and dislocating of language. But such deliberate struggle seems hardly to accord with the "direct sensuous apprehension of thought" and the ability to "feel their thought as immediately as the odour of a rose" which Eliot approvingly attributes to the metaphysical poets. These *direct* and *immediate* abilities of the metaphysical poets are, of course, functions of that "unified sensibility" which Eliot claimed for them. But when he speaks of them as being "engaged in the task of trying to find the verbal equivalent for states of mind and feeling," the poets would appear to be in pursuit of something rather than already in possession of it. Eliot's theory of the sensibilities — "unified" and "dissociated" — which has had such tremendous influence, crumbles into confusion with his later (1931) remark that a "deep fissure" was already evident in Donne's sensibility. Whatever inconsistencies and changes there may have been in the critic's theories, it is clear that the poet's sustained preoccupation has been with "the verbal equivalent for states of mind and feeling."

This idea is repeated in the criticism in various ways and at various times throughout Eliot's career. Even the famous "objective correlative" defined in "Hamlet and His Problems" (1919) has this meaning: "The only way of expressing emotion in the form of art is by finding an 'objective correlative'; in other words, a set of objects, a situation, a chain of events which shall be the formula of that *particular* emotion; such that when the external facts, which must terminate in sensory experience, are given, the emotion is immediately evoked." Although the statement is more involved, the essential meaning is the same — the poet seeks to say exactly what he means, to find "the verbal equivalent for states of mind and feeling." Eliot's purpose in defining the objective correlative was to indicate what he considered to be a failing in Shakespeare's play: "Hamlet (the man) is dominated by an emotion which is inexpressible, because it is in *excess* of the facts as they appear. . . . We must simply admit that here Shakespeare tackled a problem which proved too much for him." It is not necessary to agree with this view of *Hamlet* in order to find it impressive — indeed, fascinating. For here again Eliot is concerned with the poet's struggle to express and evoke his meaning in all its fullness. The comment on *Hamlet* is especially interesting when compared with remarks Eliot was to make, so many years later, in the *Paris Review* interview:

"I think that in the early poems it was a question of not being able to — of having more to say than one knew how to say, and having something one wanted to put into words and rhythm which one didn't have the command of words and rhythm to put in a way immediately apprehensible.

"That type of obscurity comes when the poet is still at the stage of learning how to use language. You have to say the thing the difficult way. The only alternative is not saying it at all, at that stage. By the time of *The Four Quartets*, I couldn't have written in the style of *The Waste Land*. In *The Waste Land*, I wasn't even bothering whether I understood what I was saying."

These remarks forcefully suggest that in the essay on *Hamlet* Eliot was characteristically preoccupied with his own problems as poet. Nor is it, again, necessary to agree with the remarks in order to find them valuable and meaningful. If Eliot's earlier meanings exceeded his ability to express them, then the inability was actually an essential part of the meanings — and the meanings were expressed, after all! For we have seen that so much of Eliot's meaning, so much of the "state of mind" evoked by his poetry, is the state of isolation, of the ineffable and inarticulate. It is impossible to conceive of Eliot's earlier meanings as having any measure of fullness without the intimations of the ineffable. We have seen how much this theme contributes to the continuity and the larger meaning of his work. Although Eliot contrasted the *Four Quartets* with *The Waste Land*, it is well to recall that in *East Coker* he said:

. . . one has only learnt to get the better of words
For the thing one no longer has to say, or the way in which
One is no longer disposed to say it.

Other comments made by the author of *The Waste Land* on his own poem serve to illustrate various aspects of his behavior as a critic. In "Thoughts after Lambeth" (1931) he said: ". . . when I wrote a poem called *The Waste Land* some of the more approving critics said that I had expressed the 'disillusionment of a generation,' which is nonsense. I may have expressed for them their own illusion of being disillusioned, but that did not form part of my intention." This passage has been a favorite target of Eliot's detractors, but it has also been cited justly enough by more objective critics in calling attention to the haughty posturing which at times marred his pronouncements. Eliot himself was eventually to acknowledge a distaste for the pontifical tone which occasionally appears in his earlier prose. But to return to *The Waste Land* — when the interviewer observed that "more recent critics, writing after your later poetry, found *The Waste Land* Christian," Eliot answered, "No, it wasn't part of my conscious intention." We may surmise that Eliot had his own poetry in mind when in 1951 he was discussing the poetry of Virgil. He said then that while a poet may think that he has given expression to a "private experience" but "without giving himself away," his readers may find his lines expressing "their own secret feelings . . . the exultation or despair of a generation."

Much of Eliot's later criticism and comment is concerned with readjusting his position, with recording an achieved capacity for tolerance and a catholicity of taste, and with diluting or eliminating the asperity with which he had treated various figures and issues. The essays on Tennyson, Milton, Goethe, and Kipling present such readjustments and reconsiderations. In both the prose and the poetry, Eliot has shown an increasing tendency to talk candidly about himself, and with less fear of "giving himself away." It must have been as clear to Eliot as to his readers that Harry, the protagonist of *The Family Reunion*, in his complacent suffering and arrogant isolation, was a recognizable "objective correlative" for the author — since in "Poetry and Drama" (1950), Eliot said of Harry that "my hero now strikes me as an insufferable prig." It should not be necessary to quibble about what and how much the author intended to give away in these few words. But it is well worth pondering, along with the harsh judgment of Harry, Eliot's equally sound opinion (stated in the interview) that *"The Family Reunion* is still the best of my plays in the way of poetry."

Eliot has been less concerned to publicize a readjustment of position on political and social questions than on matters of literary criticism. He has been comparatively reticent on those political pronouncements which, in the light of later history, have appeared to be in accord with Fascist programs and practices. It may at least be said for him that he was not alone in failing to envisage the brutality to which the Nazis would extend the "corrective" doctrines of the reactionary position. Closely related to some of the quasi-Fascistic pronouncements made by Eliot is the question of anti-Semitism. The distasteful portrayal of Jews in "Gerontion" and in some of the quatrains of *Poems* (1920) —

> But this or such was Bleistein's way:
> A saggy bending of the knees
> And elbows with the palms turned out,
> Chicago Semite Viennese.

— may be considered as literary grotesqueries comparable to the portraits of Sweeney and Grishkin. But the evidence of the prose is another matter. In *After Strange Gods* (1933), discussing the virtues of a regional culture and homogeneous community, he said: ". . . reasons of race and religion combine to make any large number of free-thinking Jews undesirable. . . . And a spirit of excessive tolerance is to be deprecated." The contrived allusion to Karl Marx (in 1935) as a "Jewish economist" was again an amazing lapse in dignity. Merely to assert that he was not, or is not, anti-Semitic is an insufficient reckoning with such indiscretions. But it is a well-established habit of Eliot's readers and critics to discover meanings by relating seemingly remote details from various parts of his writings. It may therefore be no excessive tolerance to apply to Eliot's earlier deprecations the splendid and moving lines, in *Little Gidding*, with which the "familiar compound ghost" describes "the gifts reserved for age":

> . . . the conscious impotence of rage
> At human folly, and the laceration
> Of laughter at what ceases to amuse.
> And last, the rending pain of re-enactment
> Of all that you have done, and been; the shame
> Of motives late revealed, and the awareness
> Of things ill done and done to others' harm
> Which once you took for exercise of virtue.
> Then fools' approval stings, and honour stains.

In 1955 Eliot said of Wordsworth, "his name marks an epoch," and it is even more true of Eliot himself. But this has already been said in various ways by various writers with various intentions. Indeed, so much has been said about the poet, dramatist, critic of literature and culture, that any effort to add a further comment can hardly escape repetitions of the familiar. And so, to end briefly with an appropriate summation and illustration of his achievement as poet and critic, it may be most fitting to follow in the convention of quoting the man himself: ". . . the best contemporary poetry can give us a feeling of excitement and a sense of fulfilment different from any sentiment aroused by even very much greater poetry of a past age." If "next year's words await another voice," it is to be hoped that the voice will be not only different from Eliot's, but equal to it in giving us excitement and fulfillment.

*1961*

# Ash Wednesday

IN HIS essay on Babbitt, T. S. Eliot has said, "Given the most highly organized and temporally powerful hierarchy, with all the powers of inquisition and punishment imaginable, still the idea of the religion is the *inner* control — the appeal not to a man's behaviour but to his soul." We may assume that a devotional poem written by Eliot will constitute a record of the poet's religious experience — the personal matter of *"inner* control." The continuity which has been often remarked as existing in Eliot's work becomes definitely apparent after a study of his longer poems. *The Waste Land* looks forward, we can see now, to such a poem as *Ash Wednesday*; especially indicative are these lines from the earlier poem:

> I sat upon the shore
> Fishing, with the arid plain behind me
> Shall I at least set my lands in order?
> London Bridge is falling down falling down
>    falling down
> *Poi s'ascose nel foco che gli affina* . . .

Setting one's lands in order amounts to approaching the practice of inner control; Cleanth Brooks observes: "The protagonist resolves to claim his tradition and rehabilitate it." In the later poem it is evident that he has been pursuing his resolution and that *Ash Wednesday* is uttered, so to speak, from *il foco che gli affina.*

In his essay on Baudelaire Eliot has implied what he considers essential for the possession — more accurately, the pursuit — of Christianity: "the greatest, the most difficult, of the Christian virtues, the virtue of humility." Significantly enough, he uses for the title of his devotional poem the name of that day in the Catholic calendar which begins a season of humility, thus indicating the tone and theme of the poem, so that Ash Wednesday comes to stand for a state of mind, a state of the soul.

The relationship which Eliot has indicated as existing between *The Waste Land* and Miss Weston's *From Ritual to Romance* is paralleled, as we shall soon observe, by that existing between *Ash Wednesday* and *The Dark Night of the Soul,* a prose work of the sixteenth-century Spanish mystic St. John of the Cross. *The Dark Night of the Soul* is a companion piece to *The Ascent of Mount Carmel,* both of which the saint wrote to expound his mystical *Stanzas of the Soul.* In each of these St. John gives counsel for the religious experience of purgation and explains that those who would attain union with God must enter a condition of the soul called the "dark night." This condition is of two stages: the dark night of sense and the dark night of spirit, in which sense and spirit respectively are purged. The *Ascent,* counsel for the active way of purgation, is intended for proficients; the *Dark Night,* counsel for the passive way, for beginners. "The passive way is that wherein the soul does nothing, and God works in the soul, and it remains, as it were, patient." It is in keeping with the theme of *Ash Wednesday,* humility, that its plan comes from the counsel for the passive way.

The statements of the speaker in section i of *Ash Wednesday* impart a sense of the debility, humility, and vexation which are to be endured by St. John's beginner, who, to enter the dark night for the purgation of desire, must achieve a "spiritual detachment from all things, whether sensual or spiritual, and a leaning on pure faith alone and an ascent thereby to God." *

*The translations from St. John that follow are by E. Allison Peers.

". . . those who at this time are going on to perfection . . .
progress by means of humility and are greatly edified, not only
thinking naught of their own affairs, but having very little satisfaction with themselves; they consider all others as far better, and
usually have a holy envy of them, and an eagerness to serve God
as these do. . . . And thus He leaves them so completely in the
dark that they know not whither to go with their sensible imagination and meditation; for they cannot advance a step in meditation,
as they were wont to do aforetime, their inward senses being sub-
merged in this night and left with such dryness that not only do
they experience no pleasure and consolation in the spiritual things
and good exercises wherein they were wont to find their delights
and pleasures, but instead, on the contrary, they find insipidity
and bitterness in the said things. . . .

"When the soul enters the dark night, it brings these kinds of
love under control. It strengthens and purifies the one, namely
that which is according to God; and the other it removes and
brings to an end; and in the beginning it causes both to be lost
sight of. . . ."

St. John's description of genuine purgation is recognizably expressed by Eliot in *Burnt Norton*:

> Descend lower, descend only
> Into the world of perpetual solitude,
> World not world, but that which is not world,
> Internal darkness, deprivation
> And destitution of all property,
> Desiccation of the world of sense,
> Evacuation of the world of fancy,
> Inoperancy of the world of spirit;
> This is the one way, and the other
> Is the same, not in movement
> But abstention from movement, while the world
>     moves
> In appetency, on its metalled ways
> Of time past and time future.

## I

The first section of *Ash Wednesday* — indeed, the whole poem —
not only reflects superficially *The Dark Night of the Soul*, but also
contains allusions which, by their contextual significance, are in

43

accord with St. John's purgational system. A structural similarity between *Ash Wednesday* and *The Waste Land* is thus suggested, for the allusions have their place in the devotional poem by sympathetic association with the idea of the *Dark Night*. A preoccupation with the purging of desire, with the condition of "Internal darkness, deprivation," etc., would bring a sharpened sensitivity to whatever might suggest the condition, would impose something of itself upon all experience and come to include within itself what has been incidentally reminiscent of the personal problem.

The opening line is a literal translation of the first line of a *ballata* by Guido Cavalcanti: *Perch'io non spero di tornar giammai.* Rossetti's translation of it begins:

> Because I think not ever to return
> Ballad, to Tuscany, —
> Go therefore thou for me
> Straight to my lady's face,
> Who, of her noble grace,
> Shall show thee courtesy.

The statements of waning vital powers, the torment to heart and soul, the condition of the "body being now so nearly dead" and of the "dead mind" make evident a correspondence between the afflictions expressed by this contemporary of Dante and the condition of St. John's beginner, whose sensitivity, both physical and spiritual, has almost ceased to function, while the soul is in a state of despair:

"For indeed, when this purgative contemplation is most severe, the soul feels very keenly the shadow of death and the lamentations of death and the pains of hell, which consists in its feeling itself to be without God, and chastised and cast out, and unworthy of Him . . . it believes that it is so with it forever."

Cavalcanti's line, as it is used in *Ash Wednesday*, performs much of its original function, for, as we shall note in dealing with later sections, the ideas of devotion to a woman and the religious experience of approaching union with God are held by Eliot in a single conceptual pattern.

In addition to the implications of devotion and distress which arise from the source of the line "Because I do not hope to turn again," there is yet another and perhaps more immediate meaning. To turn would be to depart from the state of purgation and humility and enter the state of existence of the hollow men who "go round the prickly pear." Eliot has used this turning elsewhere (at the beginning of his choruses from *The Rock* and in section v of *Ash Wednesday*) as a symbol of sterile activity and empty existence, applying it particularly to the modern world. But turning also symbolizes something else, something opposed to the sterile secular motion. The souls in Dante's *Purgatorio* are turning as they move up the winding mount which leads to heaven, the state of blessedness and divine love. In section iii of *Ash Wednesday* the turning stair represents this conception of the motion. Eliot uses these symbolic turnings in *Burnt Norton*, where he also reminds us of the *Dark Night*:

> Here is a place of disaffection
> Time before and time after
> In a dim light: neither daylight
> Investing form with lucid stillness
> *Turning shadow into transient beauty*
> *With slow rotation suggesting permanence*
> Nor darkness to purify the soul
> Emptying the sensual with deprivation
> Cleansing affection from the temporal.
> Neither plentitude nor vacancy. Only a flicker
> Over the strained time-ridden faces
> Distracted from distraction by distraction
> Filled with fancies and empty of meaning
> Tumid apathy with no concentration
> *Men and bits of paper, whirled by the cold wind*
> That blows before and after time . . .
>
> [italics mine]

The dual meaning of this turning suggests the condition of the *Dark Night*, for, by having no hope to turn, the protagonist has no hope of responding to either the worldly or the spiritual; the faculties for doing so are become incapacitated. The portions of the line which are repeated state the different shades of meaning contained in the line: the lack of hope; and the condition of being devoid of two kinds of sensibility.

A striking illustration of the sympathetic association by which allusions are present is the line "Desiring this man's gift and that man's scope," quoted with the change of one word from Shakespeare's twenty-ninth sonnet:

> When, in disgrace with fortune and men's eyes,
> I all alone beweep my outcast state,
> And trouble deaf heaven with my bootless cries,
> And look upon myself and curse my fate,
> Wishing me like to one more rich in hope,
> Featured like him, like him with friends possess'd,
> Desiring this man's art and that man's scope,
> With what I most enjoy contented least;
> Yet in these thoughts myself almost despising,
> Haply I think on thee, and then my state,
> Like to the lark at break of day arising
> From sullen earth, sings hymns at heaven's gate;
> > For thy sweet love remember'd such wealth brings
> > That then I scorn to change my state with kings.

It may be observed that the condition expressed here is in all its details consonant with the accompaniments and signs of purgation set forth by St. John of the Cross.

Although probably not a functional allusion, the "aged eagle" may have reference to the *Dark Night*. The term *old man* is often used for the unpurged condition of the soul:

". . . God makes it to die to all that is not naturally God, so that, once it is stripped and denuded of its former skin, He may begin to clothe it anew. And thus its youth is renewed like the eagle's and it is clothed with the new man, which, as the Apostle says, is according to God."

"Why should I mourn/ The vanished power of the usual reign?" implies the futility of attempting to do anything about the condition of despair and affliction. To return to the "vanished power of the usual reign" would be a regression, a return to the state that existed before purgation began. By this implication the question becomes a statement of definite religious experience, for to suffer these afflictions is, according to St. John, to be on the way toward union with God. There is no hope of knowing the "infirm glory of the positive hour" or the "one veritable transitory power," which are respectively the modes of worldly and spiritual relief. The place "where trees flower, and springs flow" is a symbol of dual meaning, representing the consolations of sense and of spirit which are attenuated by the dark night. The protagonist, oppressed by the mere self-identity and ephemeral actuality of time and place, further expresses his wretchedness by dwelling upon the static semblance of his condition:

> . . . time is always time
> And place is always and only place
> And what is actual is actual only for one time
> And only for one place . . .

The rejoicing which proceeds from this realization is a gesture of utter resignation, an acceptance of what seems to be irrevocable misery. So absolute is the hopelessness of his condition that it leads him to renounce the "blessed face" and the "voice" which symbolize hope and guidance. (The *face* and *voice* obviously refer to the "Lady" of section II, as well as Cavalcanti's lady, who, reflected by the spiritual guide of *Ash Wednesday,* is also an object of spiritual devotion in her original context.) This renunciation has a parallel in the *Dark Night.* St. John says of the soul that "since it believes . . . that its evil will never end . . . it suffers great pain and grief, since there is added to all this (because of the solitude and abandonment caused in it by this dark night), the fact that it finds no consolation or support in any instruction nor in any spiritual master." Of itself, the situation can yield no joy. One positive gesture is, however, possible: because there is nothing else he can do, the protagonist resigns himself to the situation and accepts it completely. In doing so by his own will, he dismisses the desire to strive and thus gains the satisfaction of consummating a volition. The passage ends with an emphatic restatement of the experience:

> Because I cannot hope to turn again
> Consequently I rejoice, having to construct
>   something
> Upon which to rejoice.

Such rejoicing is constructed upon the resignation to inescapable misery: the positive experience comes into being only by means of the negative experience. This is ironical — and therefore humiliating.

Then come prayer and repentance, and the expressed desire for the passive and unreflective condition counseled by St. John: beginners are "to devote themselves not at all to reasoning and meditation . . . they will be doing quite sufficient if they persevere in prayer . . . troubling not themselves, in that state, about what they shall think or meditate . . . being without anxiety . . ." This aspect of the religious experience appears with more complexity in the paradoxical words

> Teach us to care and not to care
> Teach us to sit still.

Considering the precepts of St. John, it is natural that the protagonist wishes "not to care," to be "without anxiety." On the other hand, the ultimate motive of the desire rests in an actual concern with progressing in the religious experience, for one would want to follow the precept because one really did care. The paradoxical and earnest plea comes as an achievement; it is attained by the resignation contained in the earlier passage. The protagonist would not have it to do over again and hopes that "these words answer/ For what is done, not to be done again." He would now be taught "to care and not to care" because he has made some progress along the way of purgation,

> Because these wings are no longer wings to fly
> But merely vans to beat the air
> The air which is now thoroughly small and dry
> Smaller and dryer than the will . . .

"Smaller and dryer than the will" is another echo from St. John's *Dark Night*: "To this end God is pleased to strip them of this old man . . . leaving the understanding dark, the will dry, the memory empty. . . ." The prayer and the section end with a quotation from the *Ave Maria* of Catholic ritual, words which are for the penitent who has faith.

48

## II

The purgation continues in section II, and a state (or station) of the purifying function is expressed by symbolic images, a device which Eliot commends and admires in Dante. In his essay on that poet he says, ". . . Hell is not a place but a *state* . . . Hell, though a state, is a state that can only be thought of, and perhaps only experienced, by the projection of sensory images." He also says:

"What we should consider is not so much the meaning of the images, but the reverse process, that which led a man having an idea to express it in images. We have to consider the type of mind which by nature and *practice* tended to express itself in allegory: and for a competent poet, allegory means *clear visual images*. And clear visual images are given much more intensity by having a meaning — we do not need to know what that meaning is, but in our awareness of the image we must be aware that the meaning is there too."

We may profitably follow Eliot's counsel to consider "not so much the meaning of the images, but the reverse process, that which led a man having an idea to express it in images." The idea is known to be that of purgation. We may know that the images are associated with each other and we may know that they are associated with a particular idea, but we do not know enough until we have learned upon what ground all the associations occur. When this has been learned the images will become meaningful.

We have already noted the connection between the "Lady" of section II and the lady of Cavalcanti's poem. Mario Praz remarks that the term Lady — Donna — "had quite a special connotation in Dante's circle." The *ballata* gives us an instance of the lady's function in the poetry of that circle. Worshiped with religious adoration, she is a type of the Virgin Mary, one who may bring the grace of salvation to her suitor, from whom she receives a personal devotion involving the natural and the supernatural. The sequence of the sections in *Ash Wednesday* is in part founded upon this. The Platonic lover of Cavalcanti's poem bids his soul to "worship her/ Still in her purity." Such love has a religious quality and is ironically distinct from the sexual formula which describes the performance of the typist and the "young man carbuncular" in *The Waste Land*. The most eminent instance of the love which amounts to religious worship is Dante's devotion to Beatrice. Eliot has stated the idea in his essay on Dante, speaking of the experience * in the *Vita Nuova*: "It is not, I believe, meant as a description of what he *consciously* felt on his meeting with Beatrice, but rather as a description of what that meant on mature reflection upon it . . . the love of man and woman (or for that matter of man and man) is only explained and made reasonable by the higher love, or else is simply the coupling of animals." It is probably quite valid for us to associate the Lady of *Ash Wednesday* with Beatrice, for their function is similar, although it is not necessary for the reader of *Ash Wednesday* to recall any particular appearance of Beatrice from the *Divine Comedy* in order to explain appearances of the Lady. Since Eliot's poem deals with purgation, we may take note of his remark: ". . . it is in these last cantos of the *Purgatorio*, rather than in the *Paradiso*, that Beatrice appears most clearly."

Associations of the Lady also involve the "juniper tree." "The Juniper Tree," one of Jakob Grimm's tales, is an account of a husband and wife who, having no children, but desiring one, finally acquire a boy by supernatural aid. When the wife dies in childbirth the man marries a woman who, having a daughter of her own, Marlinchen, hates the boy. She kills him, makes puddings of his flesh which she gives to her husband for food, and lies about the boy's absence. Marlinchen carries the boy's bones to a juniper tree. Then there are mist and flames, and a bird appears, singing —

*"At that moment, I say most truly that the spirit of life, which hath its dwelling in the secretest chamber of the heart, began to tremble so violently that the least pulses of my body shook therewith; and in trembling it said these words: *Ecce deus fortior me, qui veniens dominabitur mihi* ('Here is a deity stronger than I; who, coming, shall rule over me'). At that moment the animate spirit, which dwelleth in the lofty chamber whither all the senses carry their perceptions, was filled with wonder, and speaking more especially unto the spirits of the eyes, said these words: *Apparuit jam beatitudo vestra* ('Your beatitude hath now been made manifest unto you'). At that moment the natural spirit, which dwelleth there where our nourishment is administered, began to weep, and in weeping said these words: *Heu miser! quia frequenter impeditus ero deinceps* ('Alas! how often shall I be disturbed from this time forth!')." *La Vita Nuova* (Rossetti's translation).

My mother she killed me,
My father he ate me,
My sister little Marlinchen,
Gathered together all my bones,
Tied them in a silken handkerchief
Laid them beneath the juniper tree,
Kywitt, kywitt, what a beautiful bird am I!

The bird finally causes the death of the stepmother and becomes a boy again.

The Lady, by her benevolence, corresponds to the sister Marlinchen. The juniper and the bones are additional links. Moreover, the story reminds us of Christian resurrection and the eating of the boy's body parallels the Communion. Eliot's use of this story agrees with his interest in the Christian elements of anthropology manifested by *The Waste Land*. The boy has passed through death and come to life again. Eliot has used devices before to express the idea that life comes through death (cf. *The Waste Land*, "Journey of the Magi," and "A Song for Simeon"). Another source of "under a juniper tree" strikes the same note. When Elijah was threatened by Jezebel for having slain the prophets of Baal, he went into the wilderness "and came and sat down under a juniper tree: and he requested for himself that he might die." It is possible that the proffering of "my love/ To . . . the fruit of the gourd" derives from another biblical passage of the same nature. When Jonah was afflicted by the sun's heat because the gourd under which he sat had withered, "he fainted, and wished in himself to die."

The bird of Grimm's story has been carried over into the poem. It is not simply for grotesque effect that the bones happen to chirp and sing. In section IV of *Ash Wednesday* the bird sings, "Redeem the time, redeem the dream." Elsewhere in Eliot's poetry the bird and the tree occur together (cf. *The Waste Land* 1.356; *Burnt Norton* I; "Marina"). The bones in the poem reflect the tale, as well as St. John's *Dark Night*: ". . . the yearnings for God become so great in the soul that the very bones seem to be dried up by this thirst, and the natural powers to be fading away."

The book of Ezekiel is another source of the bones symbolism.

It may be observed that there are in section II several allusions to chapter 37 of Ezekiel. After the Lord has passed damning judgment upon many iniquitous peoples, he promises rehabilitation and reanimation to the Israelites. He shows to the prophet a vision symbolic of renewed vitality:

"The hand of the Lord was upon me . . . and set me down in the midst of the valley which was full of bones . . . they were very dry. And he said unto me, Son of man, can these bones live? . . . So I prophesied . . . and the bones came together . . . and the flesh came up upon them . . . but there was no breath in them. Then said he unto me, Prophesy unto the wind, prophesy, Son of man. . . . So I prophesied . . . and they lived . . . an exceeding great army.

"Then said he unto me, Son of man, these bones are the whole house of Israel: behold, they say, Our bones are dried, and our hope is lost. . . . Therefore prophesy and say unto them, Thus saith the Lord God . . . ye shall live, and I shall place you in your own land."

The chapter continues with a prophecy of the unity and blessings which God will bestow upon his people. Ezekiel ends with instructions for the dividing of the land and the negotiation of inheritance: "This is the land which ye shall divide by lot unto the tribes of Israel for inheritance, and these are their portions, saith the Lord God" (48:29).

It is significant that Eliot's first note to *The Waste Land* (l. 20, "Son of man") refers to Ezekiel. (The biblical context of this specific reference has not much importance unless we consider the entire book of Ezekiel as relative to *The Waste Land*; space forbids discussion of it.) The second note to *The Waste Land* makes a reference that applies also to section II of *Ash Wednesday*: "the burden of the grasshopper" holds the same meaning (but for a different purpose) as "the cricket no relief," both deriving from Ecclesiastes:

"And the doors shall be shut in the streets, when the sound of the grinding is low, and he shall rise up at the voice of the bird, and all the daughters of music shall be brought low; Also when they shall be afraid of that which is high, and fears shall be in the way, and the almond tree shall flourish, and the grasshopper shall be a burden, and desire shall fail: because man goeth to his long home, and the mourners go about the streets" (12:4–5).

It does not seem unlikely that the bird at whose voice "he shall rise up" is connected with the idea of Grimm's tale and Eliot's use of the bird in his poetry. The grasshopper allusion implies the failing of desire. This is an additional association with the purgational dark night, during which the affections are lost sight of.

The loss of legs, heart, and liver reflects Eliot's interest in those aspects of anthropology which seem to bear upon Christian ritual. According to the article on cannibalism in the *Encyclopedia of Religion and Ethics*, a frequent incident in folklore "is that of a child being sent out by the parent to be killed, while the assassin is ordered to bring back the victim's heart, liver, etc. . . . Grimm's story of Snow White is an instance. Here we may see a reminiscence of the practice of eating heart, liver, etc., in order to acquire the strength or soul of their owner." "The Juniper Tree" is cited as another instance. This practice and the Christian Communion are mutually reminiscent; they have become associated with the strength, the salvation, anticipated by the condition of the protagonist. The "three white leopards" which have "fed to satiety" belong to the same association. In the article "Animals" of the encyclopedia the section on the leopard relates that cannibalism and ritualistic flesh-eating are practiced by African tribes in connection with the leopard. There would not necessarily be a relevance between this article and *Ash Wednesday* were it not for an identical phrase appearing in both: "In South Africa a man who has killed a leopard remains in his hut three days; he practices continence and is *fed to satiety* [italics mine]." Although there is no special meaning brought into the poem by the coincidence of phrase with this single passage, its complete context does contain matter which recalls the Communion. The phrase and the leopards are, so to speak, handles of the association; it may very well be an unconscious one for the poet.

A quotation from chapter 3 of Genesis gives the setting of section II. When the fallen Adam and Eve hid themselves for shame of their nakedness, God walked "in the garden in the cool of the day." Besides the quality the phrase has by its allusiveness, it describes an aspect of the state, the "dream-crossed twilight," which is the subject of the poem. I remarked above that to understand the section it is necessary to learn "upon what ground all the associations occur." This "ground," as we have seen, is the idea of being purified in the purgational dark night. The images in the section, its setting, and the allusions which run through it carry the religious meaning of purgation and the way of purgation.

Eliot has said of Donne that "He knew the anguish of the marrow." As a symptom of intensity words are spoken by "that which had been contained/ In the bones." The words spoken indicate an appreciation of the benevolent guidance of the Lady, as well as the humility of the protagonist. The spiritual guide is responsible for the "brightness," which is faith. Throughout the section faith is signified by the color-symbolism of whiteness. It is by the faith which the Lady inspires that the portions rejected by the leopards are recovered. This faith brings and makes purposeful the "emptiness of the apprehensions" (the forgetfulness) which St. John declares an accompaniment of purgation.

Those familiar with the Catholic litany will appreciate the associations evoked by the solemn liturgical cadences of the words which the bones sing to the Lady of silences. The seeming contradictions which compose the passage are analogous to the paradox ("to care and not to care") upon which the religious experience revolves. The Lady is calm and reposeful by nature. But she is also distressed and worried in her solicitude for the protagonist. By being the Rose of memory and of forgetfulness she is both "Torn and most whole." (It is convenient to defer a fuller explanation of this to the treatment of section IV.) She is "Exhausted and lifegiving" in the way that Beatrice was, having passed from physical existence to become the inspiration of spiritual life. Her personality is symbolical of all the spiritual aims for which the protagonist strives; sex impulses have been sublimated into religious devotion, so that "The single Rose/ Is now the Garden/ Where all love ends." The torment of "love unsatisfied" is terminated in that it reaches its climax, the satisfaction of its impulse, by a bio-logical performance, such as the typist and the young man enact in *The Waste Land*. This performance, however, is only an inci-dent in the recurring cycle of desire and satisfaction. So long as love is merely a biological urge, forever consuming and forever desiring, there is never ultimate satisfaction. It is in this sense that we have

> The greater torment
> Of love satisfied
> End of the endless
> Journey to no end
> Conclusion of all that
> Is inconclusible
> Speech without word and
> Word of no speech . . .

The last two lines are a comment upon the emptiness and lack of spiritual meaning which belong to the love that must be forever desiring. A distinction is made between biological desire and spiritual love in *Burnt Norton*:

> Desire itself is movement
> Not in itself desirable;
> Love is itself unmoving,
> Only the cause and end of movement,
> Timeless, and undesiring . . .

The chant of the bones ends with a note of thanksgiving. In ac-cordance with the way of purgation the soul being purified is thankful for its present state, "the blessing of sand," from which the garden is to evolve. The scattered bones, shining with faith, say, "We are glad to be scattered, we did little good to each other." Much of the irony and all of the bitterness which these words may apparently contain are supplied by the reader. If the pro-tagonist *cares* really, then, according to the direction he has taken, he has good reason *not to care*.

## III

When section III was first published individually it bore the title "Som de l'Ecscalina" (summit of the stairway), a phrase taken

from the familiar *Ara vos prec* passage of the *Purgatorio* (XXVI).
The image of the stair is consistent with St. John's *Dark Night*,
in which the ladder "of living faith" is used as a symbol and illustration of the purgative contemplation. The soul "is ascending
and descending continually," experiencing exaltation and humiliation "until it has acquired perfect habits; and this ascending and
descending will cease, since the soul will have attained to God
and become united with Him, which comes to pass at the summit
of the ladder; for the ladder rests and leans upon Him." St. John
describes the ladder as consisting of ten steps. Eliot is most probably referring to these steps with "the figure of the ten stairs" in
*Burnt Norton,* and "the saint's stair" in "A Song for Simeon."

The progress of the protagonist, now signified by turning, is
objectified by the "projection of sensory images." The terms "The
same shape," "I left them twisting, turning below," and "stops
and steps of the mind over the third stair" suggest the changing
from one state of mind to another, or rather the function of a
single dynamic state of mind. The *shape* and one of *them* are in
each case the protagonist. In *Burnt Norton* the poet ponders this
movement which is "neither arrest nor movement. And do not call
it fixity." The "fetid air" is a sign of purification, representing
that which is spiritually foul and unhealthy as the issue of purgation. The cleansing process is illustrated in the *Dark Night* by
the example of fire consuming wood: ". . . it brings out and
drives away all the dark and unsightly accidents which are contrary to the nature of fire." The devil with "The deceitful face of
hope and of despair" embodies the tempting idea of departure
from the intense submission to purgation. To persist along the
way of purification it is necessary "to care and not to care." This
is no ordinary attitude; it is difficult to maintain when confronted
by the easy but futile adjustments of mere hope and despair, which
are customary and therefore dangerously attractive.

The lurid images which are suggested to the protagonist need
not be symbolical, for they occur within a symbol, one that is
dramatic: the difficult effort to ascend a stair. However, the picture called to mind for the protagonist by the passage along the

stair — "an old man's mouth drivelling, beyond repair" — reminds us of the *old man* that is being cast off by the experience.

"At the first turning of the third stair / Was a slotted window bellied like the fig's fruit." There is nothing extraordinary about the presence of the window. One is led to conceive of a tower with a window near the landing below the third flight. Whatever other meaning there may be is to this extent objectified. But a pertinent meaning is suggested. The preceding images readily connote despair; it may therefore be expected that the "deceitful face of hope" follows. The "slotted window" is, besides being superficially consistent, a sexual image. The fig is associated with lust. By taking *window* in a figurative sense one may arrive at quite a literal interpretation, if not an image: that of the female genital organ. The form of the window is a symbolic frame for the symbolic scene of beautiful sensuous images on which it opens. The "broadbacked figure" suggests a pagan fertility deity who is responsible for an appealing "Distraction, music of the flute." This sensuous beauty is hostile to the purposes of the protagonist; when it fades he gains strength. *Ash Wednesday* is again consistent with the *Dark Night*:

"For to some the angel of Satan presents himself — namely, the spirit of fornication — that he may buffet their senses with abominable and violent temptations, and may trouble their spirits with vile considerations and representations which are most visible to the imagination, which things at times are a greater affliction to them than death."

The protagonist has passed through disability of the affections, achieved some success in attaining the paradoxical position of caring and not caring, and now gains "strength beyond hope and despair." The part of man that is vexed by the foibles of hope and despair is being purged.

Catholic ritual supplies the final words of the section. In the Mass, just before the priest consumes the Body and drinks the Blood of Christ, he repeats three times this prayer, while he bows low over the chalice and patin and strikes his breast thrice: "Lord, I am not worthy that thou shouldst enter under my roof. But speak the word only, and my soul shall be healed." Besides the religious connotations which the words have, they bespeak humility and faith, and an earnest dependence upon the will of God. The protagonist is still "Climbing the third stair" — with fervor and humility.

## IV

*Ash Wednesday* may be divided into two parts, the first ending with section III. In the earlier sections the protagonist has been moving farther along through the dark night, ascending the stair according to the pattern. He reaches the third stair and is still climbing it at the end of the first part of the poem. In the last three sections he is trying to realize the causality by which he is conditioned, as well as the condition itself.

The series of questions which opens section IV implies wonder as to the identity of the Lady, the spiritual guide "who moves in the time between sleep and waking." Although the several questions imply the same answer, each of them is in terms that have a special significance. Mario Praz remarks that there is correspondence between the floral setting and the vision of Matilda in *Purgatorio* XXVIII: "a lady solitary, who went along singing, and culling flower after flower, wherewith all her path was painted." One feels urged to correlate the lines with passages in other portions of Eliot's work. "Between the violet and the violet" recalls from *The Waste Land* the "violet hour" and the "violet light." Brooks observes that violet, as a quality of the twilight, has symbolic connections with a moment of time and, also, with an experience. It may be that we have here in the violet the last link in a chain of symbols: an experience, a moment of time, a sensory quality of the moment; so that "between the violet and the violet" is ultimately synonymous with "the time between sleep and waking." It is only at such moments, under such conditions, that the protagonist can consciously seize upon the one who "made strong the fountains and made fresh the springs," for it was at such a moment that her influence was first experienced.

That these terms are put in the form of questions indicates that the protagonist has not completely established his hold upon her and has not the intimate realization which Dante had of Beatrice. Eliot expresses the belief that the sexual experience of childhood which Dante describes in the *Vita Nuova* "could only have been written around a personal experience. If so, the details do not matter: whether the lady was the Portinari or not, I do not care; it is quite as likely that she is a blind for someone else, even for a person whose name Dante may have forgotten or never known. But I cannot find it incredible that what has happened to others, should have happened to Dante with much greater intensity." The protagonist is questioning because he does not specifically remember (or visualize) the one by whom he would be led to a higher love. This is why in section II the "Lady of silences" is "Torn and most whole/ Rose of memory/ Rose of forgetfulness." These lines from "Marina" involve the same meaning:

> What is this face, less clear and clearer
> The pulse in the arm, less strong and stronger —
> Given or lent? more distant than stars and nearer
>     than the eye
>
> . . . . . . . . . . . . . . . . .
>
> I made this, I have forgotten
> And remember.

The original of the Lady, like the earthly Beatrice, was an ordinary and natural person, "Talking of trivial things." She was unaware of the effect her presence and behavior had upon the protagonist, yet the details of the experience remain significant for him, so that he imputes to her a "knowledge of eternal dolour."

The preceding sections of the poem are an account of her having made the fountains and springs of spiritual life appealing and having brought the protagonist closer to them. She has made his situation less dismal, for now the dry rock has been cooled and the sand is firm, whereas in *The Waste Land* there

> . . . is no water but only rock
> Rock and no water and the sandy road
>
> . . . . . . . . . . . . . . . . .
>
> Sweat is dry and feet are in the sand.

The words of Arnaut Daniel, the poet in purgatory, are used by the protagonist as an entreaty to the spiritual guide: *Sovegna vos* — "be mindful." Thus he expresses his desire, his willingness, to proceed further in the experience of purgation.

"Here are the years that walk between . . ." *Here* is the present condition. All the years that have passed since the first sexual-religious experience are involved in it; they have brought the condition by removing distractions, "the fiddles and the flutes." And it is only through the passage of time that this momentary experience can be recaptured, that the dreamlike person "who moves in the time between sleep and waking" can be restored. As it is stated in *Burnt Norton*, "Only through time time is conquered." The experiences and conditions recorded in the Bible, in folklore, in the writings of Dante and St. John of the Cross — "the ancient rhyme" — are restored by faith and suffering, "through a bright cloud of tears." The protagonist pleads:

> . . . Redeem
> The time. Redeem
> The unread vision in the higher dream.

We find the phrase "redeeming the time" at the end of "Thoughts after Lambeth": "The World is trying the experiment of attempting to form a civilized but non-Christian mentality. The experiment will fail; but we must be very patient in awaiting its collapse; meanwhile redeeming the time: so that the Faith may be preserved alive through the dark ages before us; to renew and rebuild civilization, and save the World from suicide." (In each case the phrase may be an echo of Ephesians 5:15 and Colossians 4:6.) "Redeem the time," then, implies a desire that such a time as was conducive to "the higher dream" be restored and the present time atoned for.

F. R. Leavis has noted that "the higher dream" is reminiscent of some remarks in Eliot's essay on Dante. Discussing the "pageantry" of the *Paradiso*, Eliot observes: "It belongs to the world of what I call the *high dream*, and the modern world seems capable only of the *low dream*." Though in the modern world the vision — which is paradise and all it stands for — is unread, this does not mean that it has been permanently lost. It belongs to a world different from the modern, one capable of the high dream, and it is this world, this time, which the protagonist wishes to be redeemed. Notice that it is not simply the dream that is requested, but the more concrete vision. The difference becomes appreciable in conjunction with Eliot's statement upon Dante's "visual imagination . . . the trick of which we have forgotten . . . a more significant, interesting, and disciplined kind of dreaming." The protagonist himself imagines a vision as an accompaniment to the redemption which he pleads: "While jewelled unicorns draw by the gilded hearse." As Leavis observes, the unicorn belongs to the world of vision, of disciplined dreaming. The image is completed with "the gilded hearse." These objects and their embellishment constitute a scene of imaginative pageantry, one that suggests, in addition to the picture, Eliot's conception of a new life attained through death. The protagonist associates the time capable of the vision in the higher dream with the ritual of the funeral. Moreover, the unicorns (creatures of the imagination) have an important function in the ritual of death — death being the eve of the wished-for life.

The supplication is, of course, addressed to the Lady. That she should be pictured "Between the yews, behind the garden god / Whose flute is breathless" and in section v as "The veiled sister between the slender / Yew trees" indicates that there is some ritualistic significance in the precise arrangement of the elements in the figure. The protagonist's reflection upon his condition is equated with the contemplation of a ritualistic symbol. The Lady's position emphasizes the difficulty with which the state is achieved, for she can be revealed thus only when the flute of the garden god has become breathless: in section iii the "music of the flute" is distraction. In other words, she becomes actual in proportion to the success of the protagonist in sublimating into religious devotion the impulses symbolized by the garden god. The yew, an evergreen, is symbolical of immortality. The Lady being placed between the trees, we may conceive her as gathering up within herself "time past and time future," in short, all reality. We find in *Burnt Norton* that past and future, though equally real with the present, are *actual* only in the present: "At the still point . . . Where past and future are gathered . . . Except for the point, the still point,/ There would be no dance, and there is only the dance." That is to say, we may approach reality only through actuality, and the Lady is here the concentrated symbol of the great past and future realities which can in no other way be perceived. The protagonist's perception of her is imperfect, however. A complete intimacy would predicate complete revelation, and she merely "bent her head and signed but spoke no word." Although she adds nothing of revelation, still she gives an encouraging sign. The fountain springs up, making secure his spiritual awareness; the bird reaffirms his petition. So long as there is no complete revelation the protagonist is right in seeking to redeem the dream, for it is a symbol of what is as yet unrevealed, the "token of the word unheard, unspoken." He must continue in purgation until he reaches that state at which the immortal and spiritual essence is entirely realized, "Till the wind shake a thousand whispers from the yew." Such is also the implication in "And after this our exile," a liturgical echo from one of the "Prayers after Low Mass": "Turn then, most gracious advocate, thine eyes of mercy towards us. And after this our exile, show unto us the blessed fruit of thy womb, Jesus."

## V

In section v the protagonist is pondering upon the *word*, the revelation which the world is resolutely incapable of receiving. Nonetheless, he says, the word exists. It is lost, spent, unheard, and unspoken only because unattained. And it is *the Word*, the very Word that the apostle John speaks of. "The centre of the silent Word" about which "the unstilled world still whirled" is equivalent to "the still point of the turning world . . . Where past and future are gathered" of *Burnt Norton*. A source of the idea is probably the point "where every *where* and every *when* is focused" of *Paradiso* XXIX. We have previously noted the whirling movement as symbolical of the world's non-Christian attitude and activity. The modern world has violated its actual relationship to the unchanging and divine essence. But the Word is not destroyed. It is still "within/ The world and for the world."

Notice that the line "O my people, what have I done unto thee" is punctuated by a period rather than a question mark. The line is from Micah 6:3: "O my people, what have I done unto thee? and wherein have I wearied thee? testify against me." These words occur also in "The Adoration of the Cross" for Good Friday, a penitential ritual. We may infer, then, that the protagonist recalls the words and exclaims them because of his religious humility and his wonder at the condition of the world. Having faith in God and the divine love, it is puzzling to him that the world should have moved "Against the Word."

He asks where the *word* shall be found, and answers himself exhaustively and emphatically, recognizing that the condition of the modern world is prohibitive of the experience which he desires. St. John's dark night is naturally suggested by the words "those who walk in darkness." The modern world does not afford the realities ("The right time and the right place") which are necessary for those who have only begun to be purged and would continue in purgation. Here in the world that is real at present there is neither "a place of grace" nor a "time to rejoice" for the partially purged, and it is inevitable that they "avoid the face" and "deny the voice." Ability to do otherwise depends not upon desire but upon condition. And the condition of the protagonist, and others like him, is that of participating in the temporal and sensual. They are of the modern world and must inescapably "walk among noise." This opinion, because one of disillusionment, is both realistic and religious. In his essay on Bradley, Eliot declares that "wisdom consists largely of scepticism and uncynical disillusion. . . . And scepticism and disillusion are a useful equipment for religious understanding." An inference of the protagonist's understanding and achievement naturally follows.

Having contemplated the circumstances, he asks whether the spiritual guide, the "veiled sister," will pray for those in the state of purgation, "those who wait/ In darkness." In enduring the contradictions which make up their paradoxical condition they are "torn on the horn," for, although they desire the divinely spiritual life, they remain unpurged of worldly inclinations. They are attracted by two opposing directions, and so are torn between the seasons, times, hours, words, and powers of the worldly and the divine: at the gate of a more spiritual life, they "will not go away and cannot pray." The protagonist pleads that the "veiled sister" intercede for them.

As in the preceding section, the Lady is pictured between yew trees. From the protagonist's humble point of view, she is offended, for the insufficiently purged would enlist her solicitude. These are terrified by the world which is hostile to their interests, and by their own apparently inalterable condition. The divinely spiritual is, of course, their highest desire, and this they "affirm before the world." But when they return to their own reality, "between the rocks," and face the chosen direction, they do not *will* to advance: their denial is implicit in their condition.

The quality of the rocks (which are red and dry in *The Waste Land*) signifies that those who have chosen the spiritual way and made some progress have gained an existence more tolerable than that from which they set out, the latter being the merely secular and sensually appetitive world. Their progress may be arrested, but they have reached the last stage at which the world is an impediment to their further advancement, "the last desert between the last blue rocks/ The desert in the garden the garden in the desert/ Of drouth." The difference between the desert and the garden is of qualitative degree. Each is contained in the other: as the purgation of the individual continues, the desert condition is evolving toward the garden condition, which is the state of spiritual salvation. Drouth, representing spiritual want, also represents the function by which all that is foreign to the spiritual is purged away. This purgation is symbolized in "spitting from the mouth the withered apple-seed," evidently an allusion to the forbidden fruit eaten by Adam and Eve. The apple-seed, withered and being spit out, symbolizes the attenuated mundane desires which are being cast off by purgation.

## VI

The first lines of the poem are repeated, except for the change of one word, as the opening lines of the final section, thus imparting formality and the quality of an expressive pattern which are characteristic of ceremonial incantation. Furthermore, this difference of one word emphasizes, by comparison with the protagonist's initial condition, the condition ultimately achieved in *Ash Wednesday*. At the first he despaired of ever being sensible to physical and spiritual attractions. But the condition has altered. He has passed through temptations and has arrived at the token, at least, of divine actuality. Now, according to his spiritual limitations and the choice he has made, his inclinations should be at a standstill. But they are not so. The purgation which has diminished the faculty for finding pleasure in the world has brought, since it was not complete, a nostalgic attraction to the pleasures that have to a great extent receded. The choice has been made and there is no question of considering the consequences in terms of reward, of "Wavering between the profit and the loss." However, though he has no desire to wish for the pleasures of the world, he inclines toward them. A confession of this follows the phrase "(Bless me father)." Among Catholics the usual form for beginning a confession is: "Bless me father; I confess to almighty God and to you, father, that I have sinned."

Attraction is exerted by the natural earth itself and its many delightful manifestations. Hence the "wide window." The nostalgic quality of the protagonist's appeal is reflected by the terms of the experience:

> And the *lost* heart stiffens and rejoices
> In the *lost* lilac and the *lost* sea voices
> And the *weak* spirit quickens to *rebel*
> For the *bent* golden-rod and the *lost* sea smell
> Quickens to *recover*
> The cry of quail and the whirling plover
> And the blind eye creates
> The empty forms between the ivory gates
> And smell *renews* the salt savour of the sandy earth.
>
> [italics mine]

The protagonist is aware that his actual need can in no way be satisfied by the phenomena of the earth, although he is, against his wish, attracted by them. This is again implied by the *"blind* eye" which creates the *"empty* forms between the ivory gates." That is, the weakened faculties of mundane conception are indulged to experience the false promises of worldly pleasures. "Ivory gates" is an allusion to the passage in the *Aeneid* where Aeneas and the Sibyl, journeying through Hades, are informed by Anchises: "Two gates of Sleep there are, whereof the one is said to be of horn, and thereby an easy outlet is given to true shades; the other gleaming with the sheen of polished ivory, but false are the dreams sent by the spirits to the world above."

The condition of the protagonist is a "brief transit" and a "time of tension" because it is not one of repose, but a straining in two opposing directions, the worldly and the spiritual. The end of the one and the beginning of the other are a twilight, a transition from one state to another. It is in this sense a condition between the death of the worldly and the birth of the spiritual, "between dying and birth." The same purgation that would utterly remove the mundane attachment would concurrently introduce one entirely spiritual. "The place of solitude where three dreams cross" is, of course, "the time of tension." Past, present, and future are the three dreams. We have previously noted that the coexistence of these is stressed in *Burnt Norton.* These times (dreams, perhaps) meet each other at one point, the transitional condition. Other terms may be substituted for these with an addition of meaning. The three times may be respectively called the conditions unpurged, partially purged, and completely purged.

The "place of solitude" is, as in the preceding section, "Between blue rocks." In the discussion of section IV it was observed that the protagonist will maintain his position until a divine revelation comes, "Till the wind shake a thousand whispers from the yew." It was also noted that the two yews between which the Lady is placed are representative of past and future times. The protagonist now pleads,

> But when the voices shaken from the yew-tree drift away
> Let the other yew be shaken and reply.

That is, "when worldly experiences and the memory of them have passed, I hope for a revelation from the divine."

*Ash Wednesday* ends with a plea to the feminine principle of spiritual guidance. The first request is clear enough; the falsehoods with which spiritual pilgrims might mock themselves are, among others, complacency, the deceits of hope and despair, the "empty forms." Recurrence of the lines

> Teach us to care and not to care
> Teach us to sit still

has the same ritualistic effect as the opening lines. In connection with the earlier instance of the plea it was observed that caring and not caring constitute the patience and humility counseled by St. John of the Cross, as well as the motivating devotion. This paradox which introduces and punctuates the poem is a motif of the purgation. We have seen how it operates in section II: the images and statements which reflect a condition of defeat are symptomatic of hope and progress. The consonance which the condition has with *The Dark Night of the Soul* saves it from ironic emphasis. "Strength beyond hope and despair" of section III is at once an attainment and a resolution of the paradox. The necessity for caring and not caring persists from one stage of purgation to another. In the final stage of *Ash Wednesday* the protagonist wishes to learn "to sit still / Even among these rocks." Out of humility and devotion he seeks to maintain patience and gratefulness for the degree of progress he has been granted. Peace may be found even in an incomplete detachment from the world, in partial purgation, by realizing that the condition is in accord with the will of God. It is with hesitation that I remark at all upon the line "Our peace in His will," which is an adaptation of Dante's well-known line "la sua voluntade è nostra pace." T. S. Eliot's own comment upon it inspires my hesitation: "And the statement of Dante seems to me *literally true*. And I confess that it has more beauty for me now, when my experience has deepened its meaning, than it did when I first read it. So I can only conclude that I cannot, in practice, wholly separate my poetic appreciation from my personal beliefs."

"Spirit of the river, spirit of the sea" suggests Aphrodite, goddess of fertility. In this symbolism the idea of fertility has been spiritualized; the protagonist seeks a spiritual birth, the divine revelation, through the solicitous intercession of the Lady. The concluding words, which are a plea for continuation of the spiritual contact, are quotations from Catholic ritual. "Suffer me not to be separated from Thee" occurs in "Devotions of the Forty Hours," Visit IV. "And let my cry come unto Thee" is the response to the versicle "O Lord, hear my prayer." The last two lines are, as they occur in the poem, dramatically emphatic of the situation. Because of all that has gone before, they issue effectually as the protagonist's utterance, their full significance including, besides their intrinsic suitability to their place in the poem, the ritualistic force and religious meaning for which they serve in a specific ceremonial performance. The individual experience of the protagonist brings him to traditional worship.

*1939*

# The Rose-Garden

THE PURPOSE of this essay is to focus attention upon a specific aspect of continuity in the poetry of T. S. Eliot. I shall attempt to follow what I believe to be an important strand, a basic and persistent theme in Eliot's poetry throughout the course of his career. Consideration of this theme may begin by first taking notice of its appearance in Eliot's prose. In his essay on Dante (1929) he discusses the experience of ecstasy in childhood described in the *Vita Nuova*:

". . . Now Dante, I believe, had experiences which seemed to him of some importance . . . important in themselves; and therefore they seemed to him to have some philosophical and impersonal value. I find in it an account of a particular kind of experience: that is, of something which had actual experience (the experience of the 'confession' in the modern sense) *and* intellectual and imaginative experience (the experience of thought and the experience of dream) as its materials; and which became a third kind. It seems to me of importance to grasp the simple fact that the *Vita Nuova* is neither a 'confession' nor an 'indiscretion' in the modern sense, nor is it a piece of Pre-Raphaelite tapestry. If you have that sense of intellectual and spiritual realities that Dante had, then a form of expression like the *Vita Nuova* cannot be classed either as 'truth' or 'fiction.'

"In the first place, the type of sexual experience which Dante describes as occurring to him at the age of nine years is by no means impossible or unique. My only doubt (in which I found myself confirmed by a distinguished psychologist) is whether it could have taken place so *late* in life as the age of nine years. The psychologist agreed with me that it is more likely to occur at about five or six years of age. It is possible that Dante developed rather late, and it is also possible that he altered the dates to employ some other significance of the number nine. But to me it appears obvious that the *Vita Nuova* could only have been written around a personal experience. If so, the details do not matter: whether the lady was the Portinari or not, I do not care; it is quite as likely that she is a blind for some one else, even for a person whose name Dante may have forgotten or never known. But I cannot find it incredible that what has happened to others should have happened to Dante with much greater intensity. . . .

"The attitude of Dante to the fundamental experience of the *Vita Nuova* can only be understood by accustoming ourselves to find meaning in the *final causes* rather than in origins. It is not, I believe, meant as a description of what he *consciously* felt on his meeting with Beatrice, but rather as a description of what that meant on mature reflection upon it. The final cause is the attraction towards God."

Several details of Eliot's comment are of particular interest to us. He ascribes an obscurity and yet peculiar reality to the experience. He regards the experience as one not uncommon among men nor restricted to any single period or kind of period in history. He acknowledges that the experience may be variously interpreted, and he himself finds it significant beyond its phenomenal and experiential details: the experience is for him derivative of a supernatural cause; it represents implicitly and symbolically meanings that are of some intellectual complexity, meanings that are philosophical and religious.

This experience and the interpretation put upon it constitute the theme which we shall observe operating by various uses throughout Eliot's writings, from his earliest poetry to his most recent. I shall try to treat the poetry, as nearly as possible, in chronological order of its appearance. According to this plan, it seems natural and profitable to begin with a consideration of the French poem "Dans le Restaurant," which appears in *Poems*

(1920). This poem is made up, until the final section, of talk made by a shabby old waiter, uncouth and repellent in manners, to a "respectable" diner, who occasionally interrupts with indignance. For my own convenience I shall translate from the French, omitting here the diner's interruptions. The words of the "garçon délabré qui n'a rien à faire":

> In my country there is rainy weather,
> Wind, much sunshine, and rain;
> There is what one calls a beggar's washday.
> . . . . . . . . . . . . . . .
> The willows drenched, and blossoms on the hedges —
> It is there, in a shower, that one takes shelter.
> I was seven, she was even younger.
> She was completely soaked, I gave her some primroses.
> . . . . . . . . . . . . . . .
> I tickled her, in order to make her laugh.
> I experienced a moment of power and ecstasy.

At this point the diner's interruption is

> Come now, old lecher, at that age . . .

But the waiter continues reminiscing:

> Sir, the fact is a hard one.
> A large dog came and bothered us;
> I was frightened, I left her halfway up the path.
> What a pity.

And now the diner finally has his say:

> Come now, you have your nerve!
> Go and wipe the streaks from your face.
> Here's my fork, scratch your head with it.
> By what right do you have experiences like mine?
> Now, here are ten sous, for the bathhouse.

Conspicuous in the words of the waiter, obviously central to the poem, is the childhood experience. Its potential significance is suggested by the intensity with which the old waiter is haunted by this experience, so haunted that he must tell of it to an unsympathetic and complete stranger. That Eliot intended the experience portrayed here as of the kind discussed in his essay on Dante is, I

believe, beyond any doubt. Its being ascribed to the undignified
old man illustrates that its source is basic in human nature and (to
follow Eliot) in a nature beyond that. This is further emphasized
by the statement of the snobbish patron: "De quel droit payes-tu
des expériences comme moi?"

In his fine analysis of *The Waste Land* Cleanth Brooks has expli-
cated the English version of the passage on the drowned Phoenician, pointing out its symbols and allusions, its several levels of
meaning.* But we should determine its coherent status in the
French poem. To observe that the passage on drowning follows
a reference to the waiter's need of a bath seems to me to be more
than simply amusing. Here, as elsewhere in Eliot's poetry, water
is symbolic of spiritual rebirth — a prerequisite of return to the
obsessive experience. The manner by which the waiter is shown
to be in need of water and the shift to the drowned man thus constitute a characteristic irony. And the shift illustrates again the
"commonness" of the experience, bringing the lives of the two
modern men and the ancient Phoenician within a single category.
The Phoenician's death is cryptically, ironically, meant as a rebirth. The undersea current (symbol of a spiritual force) carries
him "aux étapes de sa vie antérieure," presumably to an ecstatic
moment in childhood and its *final cause*. The return by stages
suggests a progress according to purification or purgation.

In "Dans le Restaurant" there are certain elements which, we
shall notice, repeatedly characterize the theme. These are the
images of water, foliage, the little girl and the proffered flowers.
Another recurrent element is the waiter's remorse — remembering
that he left the girl halfway up the path — for having withdrawn
from the situation: "C'est dommage." The more-than-scenic significance of the images is well established in poems earlier even
than "Dans le Restaurant." For example, this obtains in "La Figlia
che Piange" where, in addition to the images, there is the peculiar
quality of the departure, the "pained surprise" and "resentment"

*Cleanth Brooks, *"The Waste Land*: Critique of the Myth," in *Modern
Poetry and the Tradition* (Chapel Hill: University of North Carolina Press,
1939); reprinted in my *T. S. Eliot: A Selected Critique* (New York: Rinehart,
1948).

of the girl — conversely related to the man's remorse. The speaker of the poem is, moreover, obviously involved in the scene; his final comment on it is explicit enough:

> I should have lost a gesture and a pose.
> Sometimes these cogitations still amaze
> The troubled midnight and the noon's repose.

Other thematic elements, incidental in the earlier poems but later to be elaborated and defined, occur in "The Love Song of J. Alfred Prufrock" and "Portrait of a Lady."

> We have lingered in the chambers of the sea
> By sea-girls wreathed with seaweed red and brown
> Till human voices wake us, and we drown.

Prufrock's last words are a generalization. We bungle our adventures in the actual world because we are out of our true element, having strayed from the sea-girls and sea-chambers, the dream-world that is an approach to spiritual reality. A similar hint of the "experience" is found in the "Portrait."

> I keep my countenance,
> I remain self-possessed
> Except when a street piano, mechanical and tired
> Reiterates some worn-out common song
> With the smell of hyacinths across the garden
> Recalling things that other people have desired.
> Are these ideas right or wrong?

Here the speaker is distracted from his composure on the "actual" level by a reminder of the experience that is lost and neglected. These observations on "Prufrock" and "Portrait" are perhaps an over-reading of the poems taken singly. But I believe that they are justified in the light of later poems, and that the early passages become increasingly significant of the theme as one finds it more centrally and extensively treated in later compositions. Indeed, even the later poems will, in a sense, be over-read. Our emphasis is upon the theme, and it is often dominant in the work, but never the exclusive import — neither in "Dans le Restaurant" nor in *The Waste Land*. But on the other hand, with regard to Eliot's work as a whole, the theme is always basic as a point of view, even when actually there is no direct suggestion of the childhood experience.

In "Gerontion" the dramatic and imagistic details of the experience or any explicit references to it are not to be found. To the extent that this poem is allied with the theme, it is so allied generally and conceptually. If one recognizes the theme in the poems where its elements are more openly displayed, one will also see it as underlying "Gerontion," and consequently find that poem additionally meaningful. The title and the senility portrayed throughout — the old man — represent a sense of remoteness from the experience of sexual-religious ecstasy and its significance. A similar representation (the aged eagle) is later to be observed in the first section of *Ash Wednesday*. "Gerontion" opens with the scene of old age. Next is the statement of the coming in spring of "Christ the tiger." This, I believe, is equivalent to the *experience*. There is then the picture of Mr. Silvero, Hakagawa, etc., and their adjustment (or maladjustment) to it; and the old man again. The passage that follows is of special significance, "key" for our purposes:

> After such knowledge, what forgiveness? Think now
> History has many cunning passages, contrived corridors
> And issues, deceives with whispering ambitions,
> Guides us by vanities. Think now
> She gives when our attention is distracted
> And what she gives, gives with such supple confusions
> That the giving famishes the craving. Gives too late
> What's not believed in, or if still believed,
> In memory only, reconsidered passion. Gives too soon
> Into weak hands, what's thought can be dispensed with
> Till the refusal propagates a fear.

As I read the passage, it is a statement of the difficulty of recapturing the experience, and yet of the need to return to it; of the distractions which lead away from it. There is from this point of view a criticism of man's world, a picture of the individual's predicament. What History gives is the experience. And we find here, as elsewhere, the expression of inadequate response to it, of inability for a serious and effective attempt to reconstruct it. Further along in the poem I find the idea of removal, of the *lost experience*, even more particularized. It seems to me that this passage is an apostrophe to the girl, the Lady, the partner in the experience:

> I that was near your heart was removed therefrom
> To lose beauty in terror, terror in inquisition.
> I have lost my passion: why should I need to keep it
> Since what is kept must be adulterated?
> I have lost my sight, smell, hearing, taste and touch:
> How should I use them for your closer contact?

We shall meet again in later poems the "terror" here mentioned, and the loss of passion and the sensual faculties.

In discussing the theme as it is present in *The Waste Land* I shall not review that poem in its entirety, but refer the reader to Brooks's analysis. He will find, I believe, that the observations made here are consistent with Brooks's conclusions. The theme is evident in the first section, "The Burial of the Dead." Following the song quoted from *Tristan and Isolde* is a passage comparable in its descriptive details to the scene in "Dans le Restaurant":

> "You gave me hyacinths first a year ago;
> "They called me the hyacinth girl."
> — Yet when we came back, late, from the Hyacinth garden,
> Your arms full, and your hair wet, I could not
> Speak, and my eyes failed, I was neither
> Living nor dead, and I knew nothing,
> Looking into the heart of light, the silence.
> *Oed' und leer das Meer.*

The correspondence between the two garden scenes is surely obvious. And here, too, there is the tone of remorse. It may be noticed that the protagonist recalls not the experience in the garden, but his removal from it, his failure to see its meaning. The experience was both *life* and *death*, but its absence is neither.

The theme appears again at the end of the section, in the protagonist's speech to Stetson. In this passage the experience is attributed to all men of all times, to the man who was on King William Street and in the ships at Mylae, and attributed — with the quotation from Baudelaire — even to the reader. In addition to whatever other meanings it may have, I take the "corpse" to be a reference to the sexual-religious experience which has been neglected and repressed — or buried. (I am struck by the presence of the "Dog" here and the "gros chien" in "Dans le Restaurant," but am not prepared to make anything of it.)

The section "Death by Water," as it appears in Eliot's French poem, and its relation to the theme have been discussed above. The theme appears conspicuously again at the end of *The Waste Land*, in the passages respectively introduced by Datta, Dayadhvam, Damyata. There is first the statement of the intensity and persistent importance of the experience: "The awful daring of a moment's surrender." And then it is characterized as an unforgettable and desirable moment of freedom and communion: "I have heard the key/ Turn in the door once and turn once only." And finally the experience is again referred to in terms nostalgic and remorseful: especially significant are the words *would have responded*:

> The boat responded
> Gaily, to the hand expert with sail and oar
> The sea was calm, your heart would have responded
> Gaily, when invited, beating obedient
> To controlling hands.

I have already discussed *Ash Wednesday* at some length, indicating that the two ideas basic to the conceptual structure of the poem are the course of purgation prescribed by St. John of the Cross in his *Dark Night of the Soul*, and the principle of spiritual guidance symbolized by the "Lady" who appears prominently throughout the poem. In *Ash Wednesday* the theme which we discuss is more centrally and elaborately employed than in earlier poems, especially with regard to its religious aspect. I shall attend here only to salient points, those most obviously involved in the continuity of the theme.

The first section of *Ash Wednesday* expresses the senility and weakened sensual faculties which represent remoteness from the experience and despair of renewing it:

> Because I know I shall not know
> The one veritable transitory power . . .

The second section is addressed by the bones to the Lady. Among the abundant and complex elements of this section are those which refer to the nature of the experience, especially in the song of the bones to the "Lady of silences":

> Rose of memory
> Rose of forgetfulness
>
> .  .  .  .  .  .  .
>
> The single Rose
> Is now the Garden
> Where all loves end
> Terminate torment
> Of love unsatisfied
> The greater torment
> Of love satisfied
>
> .  .  .  .  .  .  .
>
> Grace to the Mother
> For the Garden
> Where all love ends.

The *memory* and *forgetfulness* recall Eliot's remark that "Dante may have forgotten or never known" the name of the person represented by Beatrice. This stated obscurity and elusiveness recurs in his subsequent writings. It appears again in the form of questions at the opening of the fourth section of *Ash Wednesday:* "Who walked between the violet and the violet . . ." Another passage, again from the fourth section of *Ash Wednesday*, will illustrate the manner in which the theme is dramatically and symbolically developed throughout the entire poem, as well as the significance put upon it:

> Here are the years that walk between, bearing
> Away the fiddles and the flutes, restoring
> One who moves in the time between sleep and waking . . .

The protagonist speaks from his condition of religious purgation. The present moment is seen as one resulting from and therefore containing the spiritual activity since the initial experience. This idea, it may be observed, is in accord with the coexistence of all times, as expressed elsewhere in *Ash Wednesday*, in *The Waste Land*, and in *Four Quartets*. The experience is regarded as not being subject to temporal flux but as the timeless unchanging reality. It is, nevertheless, sought and approached by temporal means. For until the experience has been re-created one must act in the world of past, present, and future. Thus, intimations of the experience, the appearance of the Lady, come under special conditions, "in the time between sleep and waking." It may be noticed that in this poem and in others such moments are always characterized by a dreamlike, twilight atmosphere, as in the final section:

> In this brief transit where the dreams cross
> The dreamcrossed twilight between birth and dying . . .

In *Ash Wednesday*, more clearly and fully than in earlier poems, restoration of the childhood experience is identified with the goal of religious life, its meaning "on mature reflection upon it . . . the attraction towards God."

Similar to *Ash Wednesday* in its basic meaning, as well as in its lyrical quality, is the poem "Marina," for which Eliot derived his "objective correlative" from Shakespeare's *Pericles*. The speaker of Eliot's poem is Pericles, Prince of Tyre, who, after years of believing that his daughter Marina is dead, finds to his amazement that she is still alive. The following passage is from the recognition scene (V. i) between father and daughter:

> PERICLES:
>
> But are you flesh and blood?
> Have you a working pulse? and are no fairy?
> Motion! Well; speak on. Where were you born?
> And wherefore call'd Marina?

The usefulness of this scene for Eliot's purposes is apparent: the unusual meeting between father and daughter is made dramatically to symbolize a restoration of the experience:

> What is this face, less clear and clearer
> The pulse in the arm, less strong and stronger —
> Given or lent? more distant than the stars and nearer
>    than the eye
>
> Whispers and small laughter between leaves and
>    hurrying feet
> Under sleep, where all the waters meet.

Obviously significant here are the dreamlike quality and the telling reference to the children among the foliage. And Eliot repeats in this poem the half-remembered character of the experience, the self-conscious effort for its re-creation:

I made this, I have forgotten
And remember
. . . . . .

Made this unknowing, half conscious, unknown, my own.

*Burnt Norton*, even more than *Ash Wednesday* — more than any other of Eliot's poems — displays clearly on its surface the spiritual quest, the constant endeavor to interpret the experience and thus to relive it. The poem is a kind of essay, including within its range scenic description of the garden and philosophic discourse on the ultimate significance of the experience. In this poem Eliot repeats in effect and amplifies the passages in his essay on Dante. *Burnt Norton* opens with a statement of the coexistence of all times, the ever-presence of past and future. An implication of this is that the lost experience of the past and the desired experience of the future are in no way repetitions, but exist identically in the timeless reality that is possibly available at any actual moment. As the first section of the poem progresses, it is granted, perhaps ironically, that the experience may not have actually occurred, may be only imagined; yet it is significantly implied that the experience is a goal to which one might *return*, as if it should have happened but did not, through a fault of human nature.

What might have been is an abstraction
Remaining a perpetual possibility
Only in a world of speculation.
What might have been and what has been
Point to one end, which is always present.
Footfalls echo in the memory
Down the passage which we did not take
Towards the door we never opened
Into the rose-garden. My words echo
Thus, in your mind.
                    But to what purpose
Disturbing the dust on a bowl of rose-leaves
I do not know.

Not having had the experience is comparable to a refusal of it; it is real for each of us, though we may not be awakened to that fact — just as God may exist despite the opinion of a world of infidels. In the next passage a bird speaks, beckoning "Into our first world," leading excitedly to the experience. But this is the "deception of the thrush," the deception of phenomenal details which seem by association to recall the experience: the scene that follows is not genuine, but mechanical and devitalized; the music is "unheard" and "hidden"; privacy is spoiled by an "unseen eyebeam" and the roses have the "look of flowers that are looked at." The details of the situation have been forcibly willed — "as our guests, accepted and accepting." For an instant the dry concrete pool is filled, the lotus rises (with sexual significance). But the pool is "water out of sunlight," a mirage, and disappears when a cloud passes over. The effort is thus one of torment, disappointing in its partial and insufficient revelation. And yet, even in such attenuated form, an intimation of the hidden experience is an unbearable strain on the limited human capacity:

> Go said the bird, for the leaves were full of children,
> Hidden excitedly, containing laughter.
> Go, go, go, said the bird: human kind
> Cannot bear very much reality.

The second section begins with a discourse upon the reconciliation of extremes; all oppositions ("forgotten wars"), all that seems disparate in life and in the universe, are finally discernible in a harmonious pattern which has issued from a single source. And this source is the "still point," describable only in paradoxical terms: "Neither from nor towards . . . neither arrest nor movement." It is comparable to, perhaps derives from, the point in *Paradiso* xxix "where every *where* and every *when* is focused." In Dante's poem the point is at the center of the nine circles representing the blessed orders, and the point itself represents the creative love of God, as it does in Eliot's poem:

> I can only say, *there* we have been: but I cannot say where.

The "experience" is, thus, allied with the point and partakes of its quality:

> . . . a grace of sense, a white light still and moving,
> *Erhebung* without motion, concentration
> Without elimination, both a new world
> And the old made explicit, understood
> In the completion of its partial ecstasy,
> The resolution of its partial horror.

This recalls the "terror" that follows the experience in "Gerontion." And here again are the hardly bearable reality and the circumstantial details of the temporal world by which it can be approached:

> Time past and time future
> Allow but a little consciousness
> To be conscious is not to be in time
> But only in time can the moment in the rose-garden,
> The moment in the arbour where the rain beat,
> The moment in the draughty church at smokefall
> Be remembered; involved with past and future.
> Only through time time is conquered.

The third section presents a picture of the barrier to the conquest of time and a means by which this barrier may be overcome. The barrier is the spiritual desolation of the world; it is to be overcome by the purgational system of St. John of the Cross — the descent into darkness and "perpetual solitude" — stated in compressed form at the end of the section.

A symbolic expression of St. John's *Dark Night* opens the fourth section: the day has been buried and the sun obscured. There follows then an eager questioning, "Will the sunflower turn to us," asking in effect whether life, rebirth, will come to one who waits in the prescribed passivity of purgation. And the section ends with an answer:

> . . . After the kingfisher's wing
> Has answered light to light, and is silent, the light is still
> At the still point of the turning world.

The "kingfisher" I associate with the Fisher King of the waste land, which will be redeemed by a divine act. The passage thus means that there will be a rebirth when, through grace, the world is restored to contact with the "still point."

Many of the elements we have often observed so far are recapitulated in the final section of *Burnt Norton*. Spiritual aims, the timeless reality which is the beginning and end of all experience, are attainable only through discipline — "by the form, the pattern" — like the discipline of art. But the world presents a hindrance to discipline: "Shrieking voices . . . voices of temptation . . . The loud lament of the disconsolate chimera." And the poem concludes reaffirming the principle with which it began, the "one end, which is always present":

> Desire itself is movement
> Not in itself desirable;
> Love is itself unmoving,
> Only the cause and end of movement,
> Timeless, and undesiring
> Except in the aspect of time
> Caught in the form of limitation
> Between un-being and being.
> Sudden in a shaft of sunlight
> Even while the dust moves
> There rises the hidden laughter
> Of children in the foliage
> Quick now, here, now, always —
> Ridiculous the waste sad time
> Stretching before and after.

A distinction is made here between appetitive pursuit and the spiritual love which is the final "satisfaction" beyond temporal activity. The "waste sad time" is all mortal time. This passage embraces the systematic range of Eliot's conceptual materials, from the childhood experience of the rose-garden to a religious and philosophic ideology.

One who is already familiar with the several aspects of this theme would surely recognize them in Eliot's play *The Family Reunion*, even upon a first reading. Apart from the superficial structure of the play — the action-plot and the family relationships — are distinguishable Harry's many remarks upon time, experience, and a special kind of consciousness, remarks which all the family but Agatha consider nonsense and insanity. As the play develops it becomes more and more apparent that Harry's problem is not whether or not he murdered his wife, a moral problem, but a spiritual problem of longer standing to which the murder is only incidental. And this is what Harry finally discovers for himself. He is beset by a peculiar need, one which his family and the world do not understand. This need is the "experience," the advance toward spiritual rebirth and the peace of religious love — variously represented throughout Eliot's poetry and described in *Burnt Norton* as the "inner freedom from the practical desire."

I shall take notice of several instances in the play which clearly echo the theme in terms which we have seen to be its most specific representation. The first of these is in the long conversation between Harry and Mary. They discuss their childhood, their most intimate attitudes; and to Harry's question — "Is the spring not an evil time, that excites us with lying voices?" — Mary responds with surprising sympathy and understanding:

> Pain is the opposite of joy
> But joy is a kind of pain
> I believe the moment of birth
> Is when we have knowledge of death
> I believe the season of birth
> Is the season of sacrifice . . .

And thus for a moment the "experience" is suggested to Harry:

> . . . You bring me news
> Of a door that opens at the end of a corridor,
> Sunlight and singing; when I had felt sure
> That every corridor only led to another,
> Or to a blank wall . . .

But Mary's brief communion with Harry soon fails, and it remains for his aunt Agatha to lead him to the door of the rose-garden.

The climactic scene of the play is the long dialogue of Harry and Agatha, in which she tells him of the loveless and bitter relationship of his father and mother, of her own love for his father whom she prevented from killing his mother, and of her emotional attachment to Harry himself. Just before giving this information Agatha introduces the motif of the "experience":

There are hours when there seems to be no past or future,
Only a present moment of pointed light
When you want to burn. When you stretch out your hand
To the flames. They only come once,
Thank God, that kind. Perhaps there is another kind,
I believe, across a whole Thibet of broken stones
That lie, fang up, a lifetime's march. I have believed this.

And after Agatha's account, Harry exclaims —

Look, I do not know why,
I feel happy for a moment, as if I had come home.
It is quite irrational, but now
I feel quite happy, as if happiness
Did not consist in getting what one wanted
Or in getting rid of what can't be got rid of
But in a different vision. This is like an end.

At this point I wish to refer to the penetrating study of *The Family Reunion* made by C. L. Barber,* whose critical judgments I accept in large part. Mr. Barber presents an extremely interesting and persuasive criticism of the play from the psychoanalytic point of view. Yet I differ with his attitude that the play cannot be meaningfully interpreted except by this approach, which is illustrated by his comment on the verses just quoted: "Just because statements like this cannot be otherwise understood, one must employ psychoanalytic interpretation to get at their content — interpretation, that is, appropriate to non-communicative, asocial psychic products. In pursuing the meaning of the play, gaps appear which cannot be bridged except by following out unconscious symbolic associations." Mr. Barber's application of the psychoanalytic terms may be wholly accurate. But I think it is evident that passages such as the one on which he comments here *are* otherwise meaningful, and meaningful as the author consciously intended. It is true that one could hardly expect an audience or reader to grasp this meaning without a special preparation, a familiarity with its repeated occurrence throughout Eliot's work. If, however, one considers the play in the light of the already established continuity, the theme

*C. L. Barber, "T. S. Eliot After Strange Gods," *Southern Review*, 6:387–416 (1940); reprinted in my *T. S. Eliot: A Selected Critique.*

is no less understandable here than elsewhere. One so prepared
would surely recognize the significance of the passage that comes
toward the end of the dialogue between Harry and Agatha:

AGATHA:

> I only looked through the little door
> When the sun was shining on the rose-garden:
> And heard in the distance tiny voices
> And then a black raven flew over.
> And then I was only my own feet walking
> Away, down a concrete corridor
> In a dead air. . . .
> . . . . . . . .

HARRY:

> In and out, in an endless drift
> Of shrieking forms in a circular desert
> . . . . . . . . . . . . .

AGATHA:

> Up and down, through the stone passages
> Of an immense and empty hospital
> . . . . . . . . . . . .

HARRY:

> To and fro, dragging my feet
> Among inner shadows in the smoky wilderness,
> . . . . . . . . . . . . . . . .

> I was not there, you were not there, only our
>     phantasms
> And what did not happen is as true as what did
>     happen,
> O my dear, and you walked through the little door
> And I ran to meet you in the rose-garden.

AGATHA:

> This is the next moment. This is the beginning.
> We do not pass twice through the same door
> Or return to the door through which we did
>     not pass.
> I have seen the first stage: relief from what
>     happened
> Is also relief from that unfulfilled craving
> Flattered in sleep and deceived in waking.
>                     You have a long journey.

85

The picture of agonized effort which is portrayed in the trancelike speeches of Harry and Agatha is that put upon one by the experience, the spiritual quest in an unsympathetic world. After the revelation by Agatha Harry is suddenly changed. Now he welcomes the presence of the Eumenides. Now it is clear to him that he "must go," that he must follow the "bright angels," which formerly he fled in horror. And thus once again Eliot invokes the paradoxical discipline of St. John's *Dark Night of the Soul.* We recall that the way to salvation begins in *Ash Wednesday* with spiritual and sensual debility, in *Burnt Norton* with the descent into darkness; and toward the end of the play it is stated in Harry's decisive words:

> Where does one go from a world of insanity?
> Somewhere on the other side of despair.
> To the worship in the desert, the thirst and deprivation,
> A stony sanctuary and a primitive altar,
> The heat of the sun and the icy vigil
> A care over lives of humble people,
> The lesson of ignorance, of incurable diseases.
> Such things are possible. It is love and terror
> Of what waits and wants me, and will not let me fall.

As I have said, I agree with Mr. Barber's critical judgments. The play has serious failings. Most important among these, it seems to me, is the degree of obscurity in which Eliot keeps his most important symbols; and also, his failure to integrate fully action and motivation with the dominant theme. Except for Harry and Agatha, none of the characters realizes what is happening. The central character's existence in a world of his own, though he admits it, prevents a true dramatic situation. The other characters do not know this world and refuse to know it. The nearest they come to it is their impersonal statement in the final Chorus of the play: "We do not like the maze in the garden, because it too closely resembles the maze in the brain." But Eliot's experiment was a bold one.

The theme, as we have followed it so far, appears in a peculiarly personal application, not related to subjects that are public and historical in the most common sense. In the earlier work the experience is simply portrayed, referred to, or reflected fragmentarily. And then in *Ash Wednesday, Burnt Norton*, and *The Family Reunion* it is developed conceptually and dramatically. In Eliot's most recent work, the poems which with *Burnt Norton* have been brought together under the title *Four Quartets*, we find the theme no less personal in its significance, but also recognizably and directly related to the social scene, the World Wars and present chaos; that is, the meaning of the theme is extended from the individual to society.

*East Coker* has been discussed with illuminating information and sound comment in an article by James Johnson Sweeney.* As a brief supplement to Sweeney's interpretation I shall indicate the presence of the "experience" in *East Coker*. The first two sections of the poem are a commentary on the cycle of history, the Renaissance, and the world today, with the conclusion that there is "only a limited value/ In the knowledge derived from experience," that the only wisdom is humility. In section III the darkness of the modern scene is equated with the spiritual darkness defined by St. John of the Cross: "let the darkness come upon you/ Which shall be the darkness of God." Thus the darkness is a prefiguring of redemption: "the darkness shall be the light, and the stillness the dancing." And the redemption, the restoration to which purgation by humility and abjectness leads, is again represented by the "experience":

> Whisper of running streams, and winter lightning.
> The wild thyme unseen and the wild strawberry,
> The laughter in the garden, echoed ecstasy
> Not lost, but requiring, pointing to the agony
> Of death and birth. You say I am repeating
> Something I have said before. I shall say it again.
> Shall I say it again? In order to arrive there,
> To arrive where you are, to get from where you are not,
>  You must go by a way wherein there is no ecstasy.

The fourth section represents the spiritual suffering by which Christian salvation is to be attained. The last section of *East Coker*

*James Johnson Sweeney, "*East Coker*: A Reading," *Southern Review*, 6:771–791 (1941); reprinted in my *T. S. Eliot: A Selected Critique*.

is a personal statement of the effort for discipline that has been made, of the meager and humble result, and yet of determination to continue, despite the increasing difficulty of the times. And now, not the "experience" alone is seen as significant of the essential reality in which *beginning* and *end* are identical, but all life, all history:

> Home is where one starts from. As we grow older
> The world becomes stranger, the pattern more
>     complicated
> Of dead and living. Not the intense moment
> Isolated, with no before and after,
> But a lifetime burning in every moment
> And not the lifetime of one man only
> But of old stones that cannot be deciphered.

The discourse on history and its relation to the "experience" and spiritual reality which was begun in *East Coker* is continued in *The Dry Salvages*. As in *East Coker*, the meaning of reality is extended beyond the experience:

> The moments of happiness — not the sense of
>     well-being,
> Fruition, fulfilment, security or affection,
> Or even a very good dinner, but the sudden illumination —
> We had the experience but missed the meaning,
> And approach to the meaning restores the experience
> In a different form, beyond any meaning
> We can assign to happiness. I have said before
> That the past experience revived in the meaning
> Is not the experience of one life only
> But of many generations — not forgetting
> Something that is probably quite ineffable:
> The backward look behind the assurance
> Of recorded history, the backward half-look
> Over the shoulder, towards the primitive terror.

The "primitive terror" is represented in the poem by three principal symbols: the river, the ocean, and the rocks, all of which seem to be controlled by secular civilization but which continue actually as menacing and destructive. I have not space here to dwell upon the full meaning of the ocean, except to indicate that, in its immense shapelessness, it represents history as other than "sequence" and "development." It is thus already symbolical at the end of *East Coker*:

> We must be still and still moving
>
> . . . . . . . . . . . .
>
> Through the dark cold and the empty desolation,
> The wave cry, the wind cry, the vast waters.

In *The Dry Salvages* the symbolism is continued with the representation as "seamen" of those who are to live into the future, and with the exclamation to them "Not fare well,/ But fare forward, voyagers." The final section of the poem repeats that the spiritual reality is approachable not alone in the ecstatic moment, but by a way of life:

> Men's curiosity searches past and future
> And clings to that dimension. But to apprehend
> The point of intersection of the timeless
> With time, is an occupation for the saint—
> No occupation either, but something given
> And taken, in a lifetime's death in love,
> Ardour and selflessness and self-surrender.
> For most of us, there is only the unattended
> Moment, the moment in and out of time,
> The distraction fit, lost in a shaft of sunlight,
> The wild thyme unseen, or the winter lightning
> Or the waterfall, or music heard so deeply
> That it is not heard at all, but you are the music
> While the music lasts.

And the poem ends affirming that life, even though it is short of saintliness and lacks the given ecstatic moment, may be meaningful and purposeful:

> . . . And right action is freedom
> From past and future also.
> For most of us, this is the aim
> Never here to be realised;
> Who are only undefeated
> Because we have gone on trying;
> We, content at the last
> If our temporal reversion nourish

(Not too far from the yew-tree)
The life of significant soil.

The three poems which follow *Burnt Norton* all make reference
to World War II. Whereas the theme in *Burnt Norton* is developed on an abstract level and with no indication of an application
other than personal, in the other poems the meaning of the theme
is enlarged, applied to particular events in history, and thus extended beyond the personal. This tendency is more pronounced
in each succeeding poem, and is most fully developed in *Little
Gidding*, which is also the poem which reflects the war most fully
and most immediately. In *Burnt Norton* the "waste sad time"
which stretches before and after the personal experience is called
ridiculous. In *The Dry Salvages* not only the personal experience
but "right action is freedom/ From past and future also." Thus
all moments and all actions can be regarded as spiritually significant, as related to the timeless reality. In this sense, as it is stated
in the final section of *Little Gidding*, "history is a pattern/ Of
timeless moments. . . . History is now and England." And in the
statement "The moment of the rose and the moment of the yew-
tree/ Are of equal duration," we see the rose-garden theme related
to time and history — for the yew-tree, symbolic of death, is also
symbolic of eternity, in which the pattern of history exists.

With the closing lines of *Little Gidding* the experience in the
rose-garden is again clearly evoked:

> Through the unknown, remembered gate
> When the last of earth left to discover
> Is that which was the beginning;
> At the source of the longest river
> The voice of the hidden waterfall
> And the children in the apple-tree
> Not known, because not looked for
> But heard, half-heard, in the stillness
> Between two waves of the sea.
> Quick now, here, now, always —
> A condition of complete simplicity
> (Costing not less than everything) . . .

This passage is rich in symbols, themes, and ideas which are the immediate materials of *Four Quartets*, and which can be followed back through all of Eliot's poetry. In this passage, as in the whole body of the poetry, the theme of the experience in the rose-garden is of central significance. We begin to see a pattern that is both intricate and intelligible when we focus our attention on this point.

*1942*

# Eliot's Critics

FEW FIGURES in contemporary literature have been so seriously and so extensively discussed as T. S. Eliot.* (How many essays on Eliot begin with a sentence to this effect!) There is scarcely an area of intellectual and literary opinion in which Eliot has not served as a subject of discussion and as a point of reference for the formulation of characteristic attitudes. In its cumulative aspect the comment on his work provides a survey of modern criticism from a perspective that is constant and specific.

In many instances the writers who have discussed Eliot are important figures by virtue of their own accomplishment, and their discussions are sometimes most significant as self-revelation. For example, the statements of William Butler Yeats and Harold J. Laski are interesting for what they reveal about the thought of these writers, as well as for what they may contribute to the evaluation of Eliot's work.

The comment is self-revealing in a still larger sense. To the extent that the voices that have spoken on Eliot are representative of the age in its literary and intellectual aspect, they show the

*This essay originally appeared as the introduction to my *T. S. Eliot: A Selected Critique* (New York: Rinehart, 1948), which contains selections from the work of many of the critics mentioned here and an extensive bibliography.

reaction of the age to its outstanding poet and most influential critic. This is not to say that many of the questions about Eliot have been settled. Since the appearance of his first poems and essays, especially since *The Sacred Wood* (1920) and *The Waste Land* (1922), Eliot has been a favorite subject of heated and vigorous contention among the literary critics. Perhaps no name was mentioned so often, and almost always the name was a cue for the critic to take a stand. While the comment is no longer so abundant or so aroused in temper, it continues to appear — at what some might call a more normal pace.

Almost every approach to Eliot implies issues which are controversial. Some of the reasons for this become apparent when he is compared to Yeats, who emerged gradually from a literary landscape which was conventional and familiar, a landscape to which he seemed to belong, however much he came to dominate it and transform it. Eliot appeared suddenly, with his "peculiarities" fully developed, soon proving unpredictable, a figure for many observers not fitting into any landscape or not even fitting together. Despite (and in some ways because of) the fact that there is so much in Yeats's work that is bizarre, private, and "invented," the consistency and continuity of the various aspects of his prose statement and poetic practice have been relatively unquestioned. His work has been regarded as self-contained, some parts significant almost wholly by reason of illuminating other parts. In contrast, the interrelatedness of Eliot's work has not been so generally acknowledged; indeed, critics range from finding it all of a piece to finding it in several unrelated pieces. A familiar complaint was well defined by Paul Elmer More, who found Eliot "cleft" into the critic of formal and traditional principles with whom he sympathized, and the poet whose "obscurity of language" and "license of metrical form" he deplored, in *Ash Wednesday* as much as in *The Waste Land*. Charges like those made by Ernest Boyd — that Eliot's "aesthetic theory bears no relation whatsoever to his practice" — and by More — that Eliot "seems to be leading us in two directions at once" — were disputed by Richard Aldington, F. R. Leavis, H. Ross Williamson, George Williamson, F. O. Matthiessen, and others. These critics would not allow that any division exists. They called witness to Eliot's consistency by careful and generous reference to his work. They showed how key terms from the criticism — tradition, objective correlative, auditory imagination, levels of meaning, fusion of thought and feeling, etc. — may be applied to the poetry, and how the favorite texts of the criticism — the French symbolist poets, the metaphysicals, the Elizabethan and Jacobean dramatists, Dante — are reflected by the poetry. Finally, they elaborated Eliot's own answer to the charge of division: that while one is concerned with ideals in criticism, one must confront actualities in the practice of poetry.

These arguments were not the last word. They did not convince, for example, such close critics as John Crowe Ransom and Yvor Winters of the unity of Eliot. Ransom, though sympathetic with much of Eliot, with his wide learning and his skepticism of popular modern values, still found a poetical Hyde and a critical Jekyll in Eliot. His early judgment that *The Waste Land* was disordered and incomplete remained unchanged, and he could find no justification for the poetry in the "conservative" criticism, which "was heavily against the drift of the poetry." Like Paul Elmer More, neither Ransom nor Winters would admit that disorder and fragmentariness are appropriate in the organization of a poem because they are the poet's subject and milieu.

While critics like Leavis, Matthiessen, and George Williamson used Eliot's criticism in support of his poetry, there were others — Louis Grudin, Wyndham Lewis, Frank Swinnerton, and more recently Ransom, Winters, and D. S. Savage — who would not allow that the criticism was free of contradictions and inconsistencies. A common judgment made — with varying emphasis — by such critics was that Eliot was at his best when dealing with specific subjects, but that he did not provide a general theory of aesthetics; and that when he did approach, or imply, the more inclusive generalizations he fell into contradictions.

If the debate over whether there is unity or division in Eliot remains unsettled, there is no doubt but that it was worth having — and even continuing. The close examination of a writer who has had the acclaim and influence of Eliot is perhaps even more valuable than it is inevitable. One of the several benefits of such an activity is to make the individual critics more cautious and reflective and also more outspoken, and to indicate the extent to which contemporary thinkers are thinking and writing in the same language. Thus far the argument suggests that they are not quite doing so — suggests that an ideal definition of terms would reveal some differences in initial premises. A difference is in fact already apparent. Often those who will not interpret Eliot's criticism as consistent with his poetry are in emphatic disagreement with one or more points in the criticism. Such disagreement is implicit (perhaps unconscious) in More, and quite explicit in Ransom. Among those who do interpret the criticism as consistent with the poetry there is little or no questioning of the criticism. Eliot's critical terms and the preoccupations of his prose are used to interpret the poetry — and quite successfully. And that is the great contribution of the votaries of the "wholeness" of Eliot. They make the kind of selection from the prose and the poetry which illuminates both — which shows that both are the product of the same sensibility, the same mind, the same personality. Eliot is a whole Eliot by identity. They have helped us enjoy and understand Eliot by proving that there is a consistency of temperament from the prose to the poetry — by approaching Eliot on his own terms; but by making Eliot his own arbiter they have not quite refuted the charges of logical inconsistency. And while accepting Eliot's critical conclusions and principles, these critics as a rule fail to commit themselves on political, sociological and religious questions which are inseparable from Eliot's whole critical position.

F. O. Matthiessen's *The Achievement of T. S. Eliot* is probably the best single introduction to Eliot's work — for certain purposes. It provides pre-eminently a general understanding of the wholeness of Eliot, of the interrelationship among the several features of his prose and poetry — by taking its cues from the prose. This is apparent in its chapter titles, which are phrases quoted either directly or in effect from Eliot's criticism. Matthiessen provides much instructive information about the poems and about Eliot's critical position. In demonstrating how Eliot lives up to his own principles and in defending those principles, he returns again and again to the more important poems, but he never gives a thorough and uninterrupted analysis of any of them (until the revised edition, 1947, which has two additional chapters, one on Eliot's plays and one on *Four Quartets*). The tendency of his treatment is to provide a general orientation to all of Eliot's work, to establish a sympathy with Eliot's intentions and an appreciation of the extent to which they are achieved. This tendency is more or less common to all the defenders of Eliot's unity and makes their comment more interpretive than judicial. A later example of such treatment is found in Ronald Peacock's *The Poet in the Theatre*, where *Murder in the Cathedral* and *The Family Reunion* are assessed by Eliot's own principles.

For all its contribution, such sympathetic treatment is open to objection — objection that it is begging the question and reaffirming what Eliot has already affirmed. Objection has been made not only to the logical basis and general limitation of this kind of treatment, but to the frequent tone of pious righteousness and *me too* snobbishness with which Eliot is echoed. Matthiessen has noted this tone in one of his fellow critics: "Mr. Leavis's interpretation of Eliot . . . suffers from a certain over-intensity. He seems to be writing continually on the defensive as though he were the apostle of modern art to an unappreciative world. As a result his criticism, though eager, is somewhat wanting in balance and perspective." Similar charges might be brought against critics like Bonamy Dobrée, George Williamson, H. Ross Williamson and Matthiessen himself. An extreme example of the strained and precious deference toward Eliot practiced by these critics may be found in H. Ross Williamson. The second chapter of his book on Eliot is called "The Man Behind the Poetry" and opens with a quotation of Eliot's entry in *Who's Who* (1932). "These things constitute everything about the man behind the poetry that it is necessary to know or mannerly to inquire." With this pronouncement the man behind the perfect manners completes the "necessary" one-page chapter. It is only fair to add that since *New Bearings in English Poetry* and *The Achievement of T. S. Eliot*, both Leavis and Matthiessen have discussed Eliot with greater independence of judgment but not with less respect and appreciation. We should remember, too, that the criticism which "suffers from a certain over-intensity" was written at a time when there was over-intensity on both sides and the outcome of the battle was still in doubt. Among the more sympathetic interpreters of Eliot's poetry and criticism, R. P. Blackmur is distinguished in this respect. His acceptance or rejection of any of the elements in Eliot's position has had scarcely any effect on the tone of his comment. The intensity of his appreciation is supported by the originality of his insights and definitions and his objective analysis of Eliot's insights and definitions. It is Blackmur's kind of criticism which is most likely to be persuasive where persuasion is possible.

A frequent issue in much of the controversy over Eliot has been his influence as poet and critic. Rarely, if ever, has a writer been considered with so much attention to his place in and effect on literary history while the history was still being made. It has been often noted as remarkable that Eliot became an influence so early in his career and that so meager a body of writing should have provided such a strong and widespread effect. Those who admired Eliot without reservations and defended his wholeness and self-consistency hailed his influence as entirely beneficial, while those who saw contradictions in Eliot and/or were annoyed with the tone of his most ardent votaries questioned the effects of his influence and in some cases utterly deplored it. An article by Sherry Mangan (in *Pagany*, Spring 1930) develops a characteristic attitude which is expressed clearly enough in its title: "A Note: On the Somewhat Premature Apotheosis of Thomas Stearns Eliot." The same general attitude is reflected by G. W. Stonier's use of the term *Eliotism* in his article, "Eliot and the Plain Reader" (*Gog-Magog*, 1933). Frank Swinnerton in 1935 wondered whether Eliot's influence had not been more harmful than beneficial, and in 1943 Yvor Winters saw it as "the most dangerous and nearly the least defensible of our time." The strong feeling with which Eliot's influence was debated may be represented by quotation from an exchange of verbal blows between I. M. Parsons and Rebecca West in the pages of the *Spectator* in 1932:

*I. M. Parsons*: "It is not only that Mr. Eliot's prose has a quality, a texture, which stamps it at once as the product of an adult and trained sensibility: others besides he can justly lay claim to that. It is not even that he has been instrumental in rehabilitating the work of certain great writers of the past, though that alone is an achievement for which he deserves our gratitude, and one in which his powers of analysis and appreciation continually compel our admiration. It is that by his scholarship, his perception, and above all by the exact and scrupulous use of language, he has made it possible to discuss literature with a new precision and with a living vocabulary once more at one's command. It is, perhaps, even more than this, that alone among contemporary critics he has maintained a consistent standard of judgment and preserved an authentic scale of values. Just how supremely important the latter may be only those who are purblind to the plight of modern culture will fail to appreciate."

*Rebecca West*: "Mr. Parsons cannot think. But he is sure he can think because he is a follower of Mr. Eliot; and he is sure other people cannot think because they are not followers of Mr. Eliot. And he knows all the proper patter to use to impress the casual reader with the sense that he is on the right side — 'scholarship,' 'perception,' 'exact and scrupulous use of language,' 'adult and trained sensibility,' and so on. 'The plight of modern culture' is due to the prevalence of this intellectual tarantism among the young as much as to any one single cause."

At these extremes and along the whole scale between them, scores of critics have evaluated Eliot's influence.

An issue closely related to the value of his influence has been Eliot's general position — expatriate, traditionalist, aristocratic, Anglo-Catholic. When Ransom said that Eliot's success "was a greater success than an American could have had in America, or an Englishman in England, it was an international success, and pleased everybody" he must have meant, only and simply, that Eliot was very popular and much admired in the world of letters. For certainly there were many who were not pleased, and many who were pleased, but with marked reservations. A characteristic complaint was that Eliot had fled from America and the present to seek refuge in the past of Europe. In an article called "The Harvard Exiles" (1934), Dixon Wecter placed Eliot with Henry James, Henry Adams, and Santayana, men who had fled, geographically and historically, into the past. They belonged, Wecter observed with satisfied confidence, to an era that had closed. It had not closed so firmly, however, or receded so completely for some critics who shared Wecter's objections but lacked his confidence. The argument against Henry James and Eliot was a very present issue, raised with fresh force and bitterness some years later by Van Wyck Brooks's "Oliver Allston," who found Eliot's concept of tradition artificial, negative, egotistical. Ferner Nuhn, even more recently, made the same definition of Eliot's position, but he attacked it with more subtlety and a deeper understanding of Eliot's intentions. Nuhn acknowledged the brilliance of the essays and responded to the poetry; he respected "the sensibility to the position," but he insisted that Eliot's position rests on a "failure of reconciliation and integration." Criticisms similar to those of Wecter, Brooks, and Nuhn were made from a British point of view. For example, David Daiches and D. S. Savage saw something typically American, naive, and artificial in Eliot's doctrine of acquiring culture and tradition. Writers of the political left, of course, rejected rather than questioned Eliot's traditionalism, branding his work as reactionary and including him among the representatives of a decadent culture — although some of them, like Malcolm Cowley, John Strachey, Granville Hicks, and Harold J. Laski, granted the astuteness and brilliance of his literary accomplishments.

A frequent criticism of Eliot, made not only by those who from a partisan viewpoint attack his traditionalism and its political implications, is that he lacks patience with the average human qualities and sympathy for what is simply human. This observation has been made in a number of ways and it has served as the basis for a number of conclusions. Francis Fergusson, discussing "T. S. Eliot and His Impersonal Theory of Art" (1927), saw Eliot as "doomed to sterility in the effort to make art out of art" because he lacked "any sympathy with non-creative types." In seeking an explanation for the difficulty of *The Waste Land* E. M. Forster suggested that Eliot had had a vision of horror and had "declined to say so plainly" because he had underestimated "the general decency of his audience." According to Stephen Spender, the effect of Eliot's poetry — in which the bank clerk, Sweeney, Mrs. Porter, the pub conversationalists "are all part of the world of *things*" — derives from the poet's blindness "to the existence of people outside himself." For all the limitations which may be ascribed to Eliot's lack of a sense of humanity, or whatever it may be called, the response to his poetry indicates a considerable human sympathy with him. If his poetry has often been read with mixed feelings, one of the feelings has been that his sensibility to the life of his time is not uncommon, but uncommonly well articulated.

Extremely opposite judgments are a characteristic of the comment that has been made on Eliot's work. An absurd example of one extreme has been provided by Bernard De Voto. Writing during the war (*The Literary Fallacy*, 1944), he waved the flag of oversimplification in an attack on Eliot's lack of faith in humanity. De Voto rescued the typist-home-at-tea-time and the young-man-carbuncular from the indignity of *The Waste Land* to proclaim glowingly their "fortitude, sacrifice, fellowship; they were willing to die as an act of faith for the preservation of hope. They were hope, the soul and body of hope. They were staunchness, resolution, dedication. In fact they were incommensurable with what Mr. Eliot's poem said they were." Also writing during the war, Delmore Schwartz took a position at the other extreme, squarely in the line of De Voto's fire — this should and does mean, of course, that Schwartz understands Eliot's intentions. Eliot, however, becomes a strange god in Schwartz's presentation of him as an international culture hero, one of the heroic and international hallmarks being Eliot's concern with the related difficulties of making love and of having religious beliefs.

It is likely that Eliot's work — the methods and principles of his criticism and the broader implications of his poetry — will continue to serve as the specific issue for controversial comment and the development of disparate attitudes. Interpretations and analyses of his poetry, however, have tended to become more specialized, more strictly in the academic vein. Argument in such writing is seldom more than the courteous expression of differences among scholars. This situation contrasts strikingly with the welter of irate and impatient differences which followed the appearance of *The Waste Land*. The first issue of *Time* (March 3, 1923) reported the rumor that *The Waste Land* was written as a hoax, and that this possibility was considered immaterial by some of its supporters, who claimed that results, and not intentions, were the concern of literature. *Ash Wednesday* was equally successful in setting up opposing camps of bewilderment: Max Eastman called the poem an "oily puddle of emotional noises" and Conrad Aiken said that it approaches "the kind of heavenly meaninglessness which we call pure poetry." It is true, of course, that many enlightening studies were made by writers who combined scholarly analysis with the presentation of their own critical and ideological attitudes. One may notice a cooperative effort from Edmund Wilson's *Axel's Castle* (which is of abiding value), through the work of such critics as Leavis and Matthiessen, to Cleanth Brooks's extensive and detailed analysis of *The Waste Land*. While Brooks's treatment has general implications sympathetic to Eliot's position, these are always integral to his interpretation, and the occasional points of dispute raised by Brooks are all on the order of scholarly correction. Although Brooks's essay might be revised on a few points in the light of later studies, it remains the most thorough exegesis of *The Waste Land*. In recent years — the last decade, approximately — similar studies have been made of individual poems of Eliot and of specific issues relating to the poems. A few of such studies, for example, are those on *Murder in the Cathedral* by Leo Shapiro, Louis L. Martz, and Francis Fergusson; on *The Family Reunion* by Maud Bodkin and C. L. Barber; on *Four Quartets*, in whole or in part, by Helen Gardner, James Johnson Sweeney, Philip Wheelwright, and Raymond Preston. The special significance of such studies is that they are not primarily critical appraisals — although critical appraisal is often implicit in the interpretations of the poetry. These studies are significant beyond their individual contributions.

It must be obvious that in this essay I have not given an exhaustive report of all questions relating to Eliot. My intention has been to indicate, after reading the critical literature, what impressed me as the most important considerations. It will be obvious, too, that I have named here only a few of the critics that have written on Eliot. My choice has been determined not only by the limitations of space, but by the desire to achieve some economy, to present a picture that is balanced with both the intrinsically valuable and significantly representative, even if they do not always overlap.

*1948*

# Laforgue, Conrad, and Eliot

IT IS some time now since the detection of sources for the poetry of T. S. Eliot has settled into a routine. It will soon be obvious that this remark is a kind of left-handed apology for what is undertaken here. I want only, by way of introduction, to announce that I shall be making some routine detections which are, I hope, of more than routine significance. I should also announce that there are several lines of interest which will meet each other at variously distributed intersections and which at times return upon themselves.

## I

It will help make a point to set down not only the result of a detection but also part of my experience in making it, for there is a somewhat peculiar issue here. There was a stage in the experience that was like the discovery of a sure answer, but attended by considerable unsureness as to what the question should be. I was reading an English translation of a prose work of Laforgue, the "Hamlet" of his *Moralités Légendaires*, and came upon a passage that reminded me, forcibly, of Eliot's poetry. When I turned to Laforgue's French, the impression was the same. The peculiar thing was that while Laforgue's prose seemed strikingly Eliotic, it was not immediately apparent what parts of Eliot's poetry were Laforguean in this way. The passage is from Laforgue's version of the "poor Yorick" scene, where Hamlet expounds upon the corruption of the body. Here is the French, where I italicize the key passage, and also the translation of the key passage, which I have arranged, for the purpose of emphasis, in an imitation of Eliot's verse:

"Horrible, horrible, horrible! — J'ai peut-être encore vingt ans, trente ans à vivre, et j'y passerai comme les autres. Comme les autres? — Oh Tout! quelle misère, ne plus y être! — Ah! Je veux dès demain partir, m'enquérir par le monde des procédés d'embaumement les plus adamantins. — *Elles furent aussi, les petites gens de l'Histoire, apprenant à lire, se faisant les ongles, allumant chaque soir la sale lampe, amoureux, gourmands, vaniteux, fous de compliments, de poignées de mains et de baisers, vivant de cancans de clochers, disant: 'Quel temps fera-t-il demain? Voici l'hiver qui vient . . . Nous n'avons pas eu de prunes cette année.'* — Ah! tout est bien qui n'a pas de fin. Et toi, Silence, pardonne à la Terre; la petite folle ne sait trop ce qu'elle fait; au jour de la grande addition de la Conscience devant l'Idéal, elle sera étiquetée d'un piteux *idem* dans la colonne des évolutions miniatures de l'Evolution Unique, dans la colonne des quantités négligeables. — Et puis, des mots, des mots, des mots! Ce sera là ma devise tant qu'on ne m'aura pas démontré que nos langues riment bien à une réalité transcendante."

> They, too, were, the little people of History,
> Learning to read, trimming their nails,
> Lighting the dirty lamp every evening,
> In love, gluttonous, vain,
> Fond of compliments, hand-shakes, and kisses,
> Living on bell-tower gossip, saying,
> "What sort of weather shall we have tomorrow?
> Winter has really come . . .
> We have had no plums this year." *

It is, of course, well known that Laforgue was an important influence on the early stages of Eliot's poetic career. But when I looked in Eliot's work up through *The Waste Land* and *The Hol-*

*The versification is mine, but the English translation of Laforgue here and elsewhere in this essay is that of Arthur Symons in *The Symbolist Movement in Literature.*

*low Men* I could find only general qualities, what we call an assimilated and pervasive influence, nothing that could be referred
specifically to this passage of Laforgue's prose. The answer to the
question, or vice versa, came only when I looked in still later work,
and found it in "Animula":

> 'Issues from the hand of God, the simple soul'
> To a flat world of changing lights and noise,
> To light, dark, dry or damp, chilly or warm;
> Moving between the legs of tables and of chairs,
> Rising or falling, grasping at kisses and toys,
> Advancing boldly, sudden to take alarm,
> Retreating to the corner of arm and knee,
> Eager to be reassured, taking pleasure
> In the fragrant brilliance of the Christmas tree,
> Pleasure in the wind, the sunlight and the sea;
> . . . . . . . . . . . . . . .
> Issues from the hand of time the simple soul
> Irresolute and selfish, misshapen, lame,
> Unable to fare forward or retreat,
> Fearing the warm reality, the offered good,
> Denying the importunity of the blood,
> Shadow of its own shadows, spectre in its own gloom,
> Leaving disordered papers in a dusty room;
> Living first in the silence after the viaticum.

Between the passages from Laforgue and Eliot there is correspondence of subject and imagery, rhythm and tone. For me, it
was the similarity of rhythm and tone that was first felt. In each
passage there is a rhythm produced by a series of grammatically
parallel phrases. Alternation and variation of rhythm result from
the change in length of phrase from one series to another and also
from the use of single words in series. For example, in Laforgue
there are the participial phrases that begin with *apprenant, se
faisant, allumant, vivant, disant,* and in Eliot *moving, using,
grasping, advancing, retreating,* and others. Laforgue's series of
words, *amoureux, gourmands, vaniteux,* seems to find an echo in
Eliot's "Irresolute and selfish, misshapen, lame."

It is, finally, the similarity of tone that gives significance to the
mechanical parallelism of rhythmical elements, for as Eliot has

said of the music of poetry, the music does not exist without the meaning. Eliot's poem begins with a picture of childhood and ends with a picture of death, and Laforgue's passage also suggests the span of human life, from "apprenant à lire" to "au jour de la grande addition de la Conscience devant l'Idéal." Common elements are the references to people in relation to furniture and to weather and seasons. The word *silence* is used with special and similar meaning in both passages. Eliot's "after the viaticum" corresponds to Laforgue's "réalité transcendante." Common also is the view of the pathetic eagerness of human need and of man's life as petty, sordid, and vain. Laforgue's Hamlet expresses here an ambivalent attitude toward the generality of mankind, implying senses both of separateness and of identification. This ambivalence is pervasive throughout much of Eliot's work, and in the final lines of "Animula" this sense of the otherness of others is suggested by the naming of Guiterriez, Boudin, and Floret, and by "this one who made a great fortune/ And that one who went his own way" — yet there is also the sense of identification in the "Pray for *us*" of the last line — quoted, of course, with the change of *death* to *birth*, from the *Ave Maria*.

Eliot's title, "Animula" (derived from Hadrian's lines on death*), means "little soul" and it is possible that the word was associated by Eliot with *les petites gens*. The plausibility of this speculation is enhanced by other details. Some pages earlier in Laforgue's "Hamlet" there is a passage of poetry containing the line "O petite âme brave," practically the French equivalent for Hadrian's Latin. Shortly after this passage is another containing the line "Simple et sans foi comme un bonjours," adapted by Eliot in "La Figlia che Piange" as "Simple and faithless as a smile or shake of the hand." In this poem there are the lines

> As the soul leaves the body torn and bruised,
> As the mind deserts the body it has used.

*O Animula vagula, blandula,
Hospes comesque, corporis,
Que nunc abibis in loca?
Pallidula, lurida, timidula,
Nec, ut soles, dabis joca.

Hadrian is again suggested here, for he, too, speaks of the soul departing from the body. Laforgue's "Hamlet" and Hadrian's lines both appear to be part of an established and continuing association for Eliot. One may note, incidentally, a kind of blending or linkage of associations, for with the "Hamlet" connection, Ophelia is suggested as a type of *la figlia che piange*, and thus with the Hyacinth girl and the whole intricate and pervasive pattern of the rose-garden theme in Eliot's work.

Laforgue's passage is specifically echoed again in a still later work, *Murder in the Cathedral*, where the Women of Canterbury represent "les petites gens de l'Histoire." In the second Chorus of the play they describe themselves as "the small folk drawn into the pattern of fate, the small folk who live among small things." In the same Chorus they speak these lines:

> Sometimes the corn has failed us,
> Sometimes the harvest is good,
> One year is a year of rain
> Another a year of dryness,
> One year the apples are abundant,
> Another year the plums are lacking.
> Yet we have gone on living,
> Living and partly living.

Like Laforgue's *petites gens*, Eliot's small folk are concerned with weather, seasons, and crops. Both speak in a rhythm that is produced by a series of short and simple statements. It is, I think, something of a curiosity that Eliot follows Laforgue in ending the series of statements with the mention of the plums. The plums and the small folk are the kind of detail, bolstered by the context, on which one can pin one's arguments, and if it were not for the detail, one might have doubts, or at least some timidity about setting down one's impressions. This instance is a formidable lesson in how elusive the question of influence may be. For example, there may be Laforguean echoes in *Four Quartets* and Eliot's other plays, as I shall eventually suggest, but without the benefit of any "plums." *

*The general impression that Laforgue's influence ceased early in Eliot's career and that it is not shown by the plays is reflected by E. J. H. Greene's

## II

At the end of his essay "Swinburne as Poet" (1920) Eliot remarks that "the language which is more important to us is that which is struggling to digest and express new objects, new groups of objects, new feelings, new aspects, as, for instance, the prose of Mr. James Joyce or the earlier Conrad." It is the reference to Conrad with which I am concerned. As far as I know, neither Eliot himself nor anyone else has elaborated on the meaning of this statement. We have long known, of course, from the epigraph to *The Hollow Men* (" 'Mistah Kurtz — he dead' ") that *Heart of Darkness* has a general relevance to this poem. There is also the exchange of letters between Eliot and Ezra Pound at the time Pound had made his now famous criticism of Eliot's manuscript of *The Waste Land.** We learn from these letters that Eliot had originally intended to use Kurtz's dying words " 'The horror! the horror!' " as the epigraph to that poem. Pound had written Eliot, "I doubt if Conrad is weighty enough to stand the citation." Eliot replied, "Do you mean not use the Conrad quote or simply not put Conrad's name to it? It is much the most appropriate I can find, and somewhat elucidative." To this, Pound answered that Eliot should do as he liked. Although Eliot yielded the point, it is obvious from his remarks that Conrad was far weightier for him than he was for Pound.

What, then, is the relevance of *Heart of Darkness* to *The Waste Land*? There is in the first section of the poem the line "Looking into the heart of light, the silence," which contains a phrase suggestive of the title of Conrad's story. It has been noted † that the first song of the Thames-daughters,

> The barges drift
> With the turning tide

book *T. S. Eliot et la France* (Paris: Boivin, 1951): "Les œuvres dramatiques d'Eliot, *The Rock* (1934), *Murder in the Cathedral* (1935) et *The Family Reunion* (1939), ne portent pas de traces d'influence française" (p. 136).

*Eliot's letter, as well as Pound's, is printed in *The Letters of Ezra Pound 1907–1941*, edited by D. D. Paige (New York: Harcourt, Brace, 1950), pp. 169–171.

†By Elizabeth Drew, in *T. S. Eliot: The Design of His Poetry* (New York: Scribner's, 1949), pp. 91–92.

> Red sails
> Wide
> To leeward . . .

derives images from Conrad's description of the Thames at the opening of the story: "In the offing the sea and the sky were welded together without a joint, and in the luminous space the tanned sails of the barges drifting up with the tide seemed to stand still in red clusters of canvas sharply peaked, with gleams of varnished sprits." Eliot's use of these images is, however, not enough to explain why the reference to Conrad's story is "much the most appropriate I can find, and somewhat elucidative." In this respect, it is not the images but the river as a locus of history and of memory that is most significant. Conrad develops this idea in the early paragraphs of the story:

"The old river in its broad reach rested unruffled at the decline of day, after ages of good service done to the race that peopled its banks . . . We looked at the venerable stream not in the vivid flush of a short day that comes and departs forever, but in the august light of abiding memories. And indeed nothing is easier . . . than to evoke the great spirit of the past upon the lower reaches of the Thames. The tidal current runs to and fro in its unceasing service, crowded with memories of men and ships it had borne to the rest of home or to the battles of the sea."

After this come evocative allusions to English sea-history and its role in the development of empire. Then Marlow begins his long talk to his mates with the remarks:

"'And this also . . . has been one of the dark places of the earth. . . . I was thinking of very old times, when the Romans first came here, nineteen hundred years ago—the other day. . . . Light came out of this river since—you say knights? Yes; but it is like a running blaze on a plain, like a flash of lightning in the clouds. We live in the flicker—may it last as long as the old earth keeps rolling! But darkness was here yesterday.'"

Marlow goes on to imagine the experience of the Romans who encountered the savagery and mystery of ancient England, "'the growing regrets, the longing to escape, the powerless disgust, the surrender, the hate.'" He evokes the ancient experience not only with great vividness, but gives it a quality of the contemporaneous, rendering the past in terms of the present — " 'their administration was merely a squeeze, and nothing more, I suspect.' " This part of the story is in thematic relationship with Conrad's evocation of England's glorious sea-history and also with the tale that Marlow is to tell of his journey on another river in search of Mr. Kurtz and into the heart of darkness.

One of my purposes (others will appear) in quoting and reviewing this much of the story is to indicate a facet of relationship between the story and the poem. In both there are the "abiding memories" and "spirit of the past." Eliot's intricate and complex merging of times, places, and persons may not have been suggested by Conrad's story, but the story is in this respect appropriate and elucidative. Later in the story Marlow makes a comment which states a major theme of Eliot's poetry and a frequent preoccupation of his prose: " 'The mind of man is capable of anything — because everything is in it, all the past as well as all the future.' " The water imagery of both works is involved in this theme. Conrad develops his theme of time and history with relation to the Thames and then suggests a relation between the Thames — "darkness was here yesterday" — and the African river where yesterday's darkness still exists. In *The Waste Land* times and places are merged with reference to rivers and seaways: "You who were with me in the ships at Mylae!" "By the waters of Leman I sat down and wept."

There are other ways in which *Heart of Darkness* can be brought to bear upon *The Waste Land*, but since I believe that the story is also related to Eliot's later development, it is a convenient and economical strategy to say so at this time. In order to treat this subject, I shall have to quote at some length. After the account of Kurtz's death, Marlow tells of his own almost fatal illness and then of his return to the European city:

" 'However, as you see, I did not go to join Kurtz there and then. I did not. I remained to dream the nightmare out to the end, and to show my loyalty to Kurtz once more. Destiny. My destiny! Droll thing life is — that mysterious arrangement of merciless logic for a futile purpose. The most you can hope from it is some knowledge of yourself — that comes too late — a crop of unextinguishable regrets. I have wrestled with death. It is the most unexciting contest you can imagine. It takes place in an impalpable grayness, with nothing underfoot, with nothing around, without spectators, without clamor, without glory, without the great desire of victory, without the great fear of defeat, in a sickly atmosphere of tepid skepticism, without much belief in your own right, and still less in that of your adversary. If such is the form of ultimate wisdom, then life is a greater riddle than some of us think it to be. I was within a hair's-breadth of the last opportunity for pronouncement, and I found with humiliation that probably I would have nothing to say. This is the reason why I affirm that Kurtz was a remarkable man. He had something to say. He said it. Since I had peeped over the edge myself, I understand better the meaning of his stare, that could not see the flame of the candle but was wide enough to embrace the whole universe, piercing enough to penetrate all the hearts that beat in the darkness. He had summed up — he had judged. "The horror!" He was a remarkable man. After all, this was the expression of some sort of belief; it had candor, it had conviction, it had a vibrating note of revolt in its whisper, it had the appalling face of a glimpsed truth — the strange commingling of desire and hate. And it is not my own extremity I remember best — a vision of grayness without form filled with physical pain, and a careless contempt for the evanescence of all things — even of this pain itself. No! It is his extremity that I seem to have lived through. True, he had made that last stride, he had stepped over the edge, while I had been permitted to draw back my hesitating foot. And perhaps in this is the whole difference; perhaps all the wisdom, and all truth, and all sincerity, are just compressed into that inappreciable moment of time in which we step over the threshold of the invisible. Perhaps! I like to think my summing up would not have been a word of careless contempt. Better his cry — much better. It was an affirmation, a moral victory paid for by innumerable defeats, by abominable terrors, by abominable satisfactions. But it was a victory! That is why I have remained loyal to Kurtz to the last, and even beyond, when a long time after I heard once more, not his own voice, but the echo of his magnificent eloquence thrown to me from a soul as translucently pure as a cliff of crystal.

" 'No, they did not bury me, though there is a period of time which I remember mistily, with a shuddering wonder, like a passage through some inconceivable world that had no hope in it and no desire. I found myself back in the sepulchral city resenting the sight of people hurrying through the streets to filch a little money from each other, to devour their infamous cookery, to gulp their unwholesome beer, to dream their insignificant and silly dreams. They trespassed upon my thoughts. They were intruders whose knowledge of life was to me an irritating pretense, because I felt so sure they could not possibly know the things I knew. Their bearing, which was simply the bearing of commonplace individuals going about their business in the assurance of perfect safety, was offensive to me like the outrageous flauntings of folly in the face of a danger it is unable to comprehend. I had no particular desire to enlighten them, but I had some difficulty in restraining myself from laughing in their faces, so full of stupid importance. I dare say I was not very well at that time.' "

The first issue I shall raise about this passage is that of the language, which Eliot found so important in the earlier Conrad. I shall find it helpful to refer again to my own experience. Long familiar with the story, at a particular rereading I found myself hearing in this passage the accents and inflections, the familiar voice, of Eliot's poetry. The situation was like the one I had encountered with Laforgue's "Hamlet" — but of course, with some differences, and these differences become difficulties here. The story is widely known and the passage is fairly often cited in comments on Eliot, where some of the attitudes and ideas expressed by Marlow are related to *The Hollow Men* and *The Waste Land*. I was aware of all this, and had for long regarded the passage as impressively Conradian. How, then, shall I ask the reader to acknowledge what I now see and hear, and what I feel, in the passage?

Perhaps it is already evident, but there may nonetheless be some purpose in pursuing the question. Hoping to emphasize the Eliotic qualities of Conrad's prose, I shall arrange parts of it in an imitation of Eliot's verse.

> It takes place in an impalpable grayness,
> With nothing underfoot, with nothing around,
> Without spectators, without clamor, without glory,
> Without the great desire of victory,
> Without the great fear of defeat,

In a sickly atmosphere of tepid skepticism,
Without much belief in your own right,
And still less in that of your adversary.

No, they did not bury me,
Though there is a period of time
Which I remember mistily, with a shuddering
    wonder,
Like a passage through some inconceivable world
That had no hope in it and no desire.
I found myself back in the sepulchral city
Resenting the sight of people hurrying through
    the streets
To filch a little money from each other,
To devour their infamous cookery,
To gulp their unwholesome beer,
To dream their insignificant and silly dreams.
They trespassed upon my thoughts.

As in the case of Laforgue, we must ask, What parts of Eliot's
poetry are Conradian in this way? Since *The Waste Land* and
*The Hollow Men* have a documented relationship to the story,
I shall look at these poems first. In both these excerpts, and especially in the first, there are the negativity, the vacuity, the lack of
desire, and the "tepid skepticism" which also inform the opening
lines of *The Waste Land* and the whole of *The Hollow Men*.
There are other, and perhaps more specific, elements of correspondence: In *The Waste Land*, between "A crowd flowed over
London Bridge, so many" and Conrad's "the sight of people
hurrying through the streets"; between "I had not thought death
had undone so many" and Conrad's "sepulchral city"; between
"Unreal City" and Conrad's "some inconceivable world." In *The
Hollow Men*, between "shade without colour," "the twilight king-
dom," and Conrad's "an impalpable grayness." These correspondences of image and idea no doubt contribute to the similarity of
sound between Eliot and Conrad, yet they do not wholly explain
it. But before going on to this question I should like to call
attention to elements in Eliot's earlier work that may echo in the
reading of Conrad. I refer to "Preludes" and note these corre-

spondences: "smell of steaks" with "infamous cookery"; "smells of beer" with "unwholesome beer"; "the sawdust-trampled street" with "hurrying through the streets"; "early coffee-stands" and "a thousand furnished rooms" (by implication) with "to filch a little money from each other"; "the night revealing/ The thousand sordid images/ Of which your soul was constituted" with "to dream their insignificant and silly dreams"; "eyes/ Assured of certain certainties" with "the assurance of perfect safety" and "their faces, so full of stupid importance." Finally, Eliot's poem and the passage from Conrad both end with images of grotesque laughter. It is to be noted that both writers depict the cycle of activities of the ordinary day, and that the corresponding elements are in an approximately corresponding order.

Turning now strictly to the question of sound, we can note in the versified excerpts from Conrad not only images and ideas like those of Eliot, but also rhythmical patterns like those of Eliot's verse. In fact, it so happens that Conrad's rhythmical devices are precisely those we noticed in Laforgue's prose and in the passages of Eliot that are allied to it. These devices are series of parallel and grammatically limited phrases, with alternation and variation of rhythm produced from series to series by differing lengths and constructions of phrase. The most obvious features of this kind in the excerpts from Conrad are the prepositional and infinitive phrases. But where else in Eliot do we find this rhythmical pattern? It is present throughout *The Hollow Men* and *Ash Wednesday* and it is common in *The Waste Land*, where an obvious example is the opening passage, with its participial phrases beginning with *breeding, mixing, stirring, covering, feeding*. Another example may be found near the end of the poem:

> My friend, blood shaking my heart
> The awful daring of a moment's surrender
> Which an age of prudence can never retract
> By this, and this only, we have existed
> Which is not to be found in our obituaries
> Or in memories draped by the beneficent spider
> Or under seals broken by the lean solicitor
> In our empty rooms.

Indeed, I find the pattern common throughout the entire body
of Eliot's poetry, but I shall illustrate, with rigorous selection, only
from the later work.

> Where there is no temple there shall be no homes,
> Though you have shelters and institutions,
> Precarious lodgings while the rent is paid,
> Subsiding basements where the rat breeds
> Or sanitary dwellings with numbered doors
> Or a house a little better than your neighbors . . .
>
> *The Rock*

> . . . Only a flicker
> Over the strained time-ridden faces
> Distracted from distraction by distraction
> Filled with fancies and empty of meaning
> Tumid apathy with no concentration
> Men and bits of paper, whirled by the cold wind
> That blows before and after time . . .
>
> *Burnt Norton*

> . . . a time
> Older than the time of chronometers, older
> Than time counted by anxious worried women
> Lying awake, calculating the future,
> Trying to unweave, unwind, unravel
> And piece together the past and the future . . .
>
> *The Dry Salvages*

Emptiness, absence, separation from God;
The horror of the effortless journey to the empty land
Which is no land, only emptiness, absence, the Void,
Where those who were men can no longer turn the mind
To distraction, delusion, escape into dream, pretence
Where the soul is no longer deceived, for there are
  no objects, no tones,
No colours, no forms to distract, to divert the soul
From seeing itself, foully united forever, nothing
  with nothing . . .

> *Murder in the Cathedral*

The sudden solitude in a crowded desert
In a thick smoke, many creatures moving
Without direction, for no direction

Leads anywhere but round and round in that vapour —
Without purpose, and without principle of conduct
In flickering intervals of light and darkness;
The partial anaesthesia of suffering without feeling
And partial observation of one's own automatism
While the slow stain sinks deeper through the skin
Tainting the flesh and discolouring the bone . . .

*The Family Reunion*

. . . They may remember
The vision they have had, but they cease to regret it,
Maintain themselves by the common routine,
Learn to avoid excessive expectation,
Become tolerant of themselves and others,
Giving and taking, in the usual actions
What there is to give and take. They do not repine;
Are contented with the morning that separates
And with the evening that brings together
For casual talk before the fire
Two people who know they do not understand each other,
Breeding children whom they do not understand
And who will never understand them.

*The Cocktail Party*

I know what you mean. Then the flowers would fade
And the music would stop. And the walls would be broken.
And you would find yourself in a devastated area —
A bomb-site . . . willow-herb . . . a dirty public square.

*The Confidential Clerk*

A peculiar problem that has perhaps been pressing for some
time arises from Eliot's having this characteristic rhythm in common both with Laforgue and Conrad. It is, indeed, curious that
these two writers are, in the passages indicated, reminiscent of
Eliot in the same way, and thus reminiscent also of each other.
My own experience tells me that a reader familiar with Eliot
might project Eliotic qualities onto the passages of Laforgue and
Conrad, but this is possible because there is actually a coincidence
of elements between the two passages. In addition to the common
rhythmical patterns already noted, there are also a number of
similar meanings. Laforgue's Hamlet and Conrad's Marlow both

express attitudes of alienation from the ordinary routines of human existence, routines which they both evoke with comparable details and qualities. Each speaker is preoccupied with death and, moreover, with the moment of death. Almost immediately after the passage quoted from Laforgue, Hamlet makes this comment: "Mourir! C'est entendu, on meurt sans s'en apercevoir, comme chaque soir on entre en sommeil. On n'a pas conscience du passage de la dernière pensée lucide au sommeil, à la syncope, à la Mort." ("To die! Evidently, one dies without knowing it, as, every night, one enters upon sleep. One has no consciousness of the passing of the last lucid thought into sleep, into swooning, into death.")

And this corresponds, of course, to Marlow's " 'I was within a hair's-breadth of the last opportunity for pronouncement, and I found with humiliation that probably I would have nothing to say.' " All these correspondences between Laforgue and Conrad are sufficient to suggest that Eliot has been aware of them, although with what degree of consciousness I am not prepared to say. My speculation is that the stories of Laforgue and Conrad struck in Eliot an already existing chord, and that this chord has reverberated throughout his work. Eliot has made a number of remarks which support this notion. In the first he is speaking of imagery borrowed by Chapman, in his *Bussy d'Ambois*, from Seneca:

"There is first the probability that this imagery had some personal saturation value, so to speak, for Seneca; another for Chapman, and another for myself, who have borrowed it twice from Chapman. I suggest that what gives it such intensity as it has in each case is its saturation — I will not say with 'associations,' for I do not want to revert to Hartley — but with feelings too obscure for the authors even to know quite what they were." (*The Use of Poetry and the Use of Criticism.*)

\* \* \*

"I know that a poem, or a passage of a poem, may tend to realize itself first as a particular rhythm before it reaches expression in words, and that this rhythm may bring to birth the idea and the image; and I do not believe that this is an experience peculiar to myself." ("The Music of Poetry.")

These remarks, taken together, indicate that certain rhythms and images have had for Eliot a profound and abiding personal value, that they have been involved with feelings and ideas, and that all have been in a poetically creative relationship. Another and more general correspondence between Laforgue and Conrad, and one that would be significant to Eliot, lies in the fact that both passages are *spoken* (by Hamlet and Marlow) and show the qualities of the idiom to which Eliot has more than once said poetry must at times return. Closely relevant also is his remark that "poetry has as much to learn from prose as from other poetry; and I think that an interaction between prose and verse, like the interaction between language and language, is a condition of vitality in literature" (*The Use of Poetry and the Use of Criticism*). It is also conceivable that the passages by Laforgue and Conrad impressed Eliot and became associated for him because, among other reasons, they both show that pattern of rhythm which is characteristic of the poetry of the Bible. Any familiar passage — the Twenty-Third Psalm — will illustrate. A convention of ancient Hebrew poetry, arising out of the very nature of the language, is a rhythm that is logical and grammatical rather than syllabic. This rhythm survives in translation because it is basically a rhythm of thought, of statements simply made in a succession of grammatically parallel constructions — a rhythm that arises from the nature of human utterance itself. Writers of free verse, beginning with Whitman, have often turned to this mode of rhythm as an alternative to the rhythm of metered syllables. The Bible echoes and re-echoes in Eliot's poetry, and frequently it is the device of rhythm which produces the echo. At times the style is actually biblical, and at times it is a blending of biblical and contemporary idioms, as in these lines from *The Rock*:

> . . . In this land
> There shall be one cigarette to two men,
> To two women one half pint of bitter
> Ale. In this land
> No man has hired us.
> Our life is unwelcome, our death
> Unmentioned in "The Times."

### III

The list of quotations from Eliot's poetry given above illustrates the persistence of a rhythmical pattern, but I should like to explore further other kinds of reverberation of the chord struck by Laforgue and Conrad, and at times with attention to some of these quotations. Recalling Marlow's remark " 'We live in the flicker,' " we may note the presence of this image in the passage from *Burnt Norton* — "Only a flicker/ Over the strained time-ridden faces," and from *The Family Reunion* — "In flickering intervals of light and darkness." In the passage from *The Cocktail Party* the same image of the alternation of nights and days is suggested by "the morning that separates/ And . . . the evening that brings together." This image of recurring alternation is also to be found in the earlier work, as in the sequence from evening to morning to evening in "Preludes," and in *Sweeney Agonistes*,

> And the morning
> And the evening
> And noontime
> And night
> Morning
> Evening
> Noontime
> Night . . .

These earlier instances might more plausibly be considered facets of the already existing chord rather than of the effected reverberation.

Turning now to the passage from *Murder in the Cathedral*, we find in this picture of unredeemed death a detailed correspondence with Marlow's account of his illness and of his return to "the sepulchral city." "The effortless journey, to the empty land/ Which is no land, only emptiness, absence, the Void" is indeed "like a passage through some inconceivable world that had no hope in it and no desire." The words *dream* and *pretense* occur in both passages with similar value. The condition of "no objects, no tones,/ No colours, no forms to distract, to divert the soul/ From seeing itself, foully united forever, nothing with nothing," is like the condition of "an impalpable grayness, with nothing underfoot, with nothing around, without spectators, without clamor, without glory" — and is also the condition of having "nothing to say" at the "last opportunity for pronouncement." We find in these lines of the Chorus the idea of the moment of death, which is common to both Laforgue and Conrad and which appears elsewhere in Eliot's work. In *The Family Reunion* Amy, Harry's mother, remarks to his aunts and uncles,

> You none of you understand how old you are
> And death will come to you as a mild surprise,
> A momentary shudder in a vacant room.

The implication in every case is that the essential quality of the moment of death is also the essential quality of the individual in all his living. This idea is stated explicitly, with a quotation from the *Baghavad Gita*, in *The Dry Salvages*:

> At the moment which is not of action or inaction
> You can receive this: 'on whatever sphere of being
> The mind of man may be intent
> At the time of death' — that is the one action
> (And the time of death is every moment)
> Which shall fructify in the lives of others.

In the light of this, we may recall Marlow's loyalty to the remarkable Kurtz, and Marlow's statement: "'. . . perhaps all the wisdom, and all truth, and all sincerity, are just compressed into that inappreciable moment of time in which we step over the threshold of the invisible.'"

There is some ambiguity in Marlow's use of the word *flicker*, or perhaps I have created this ambiguity by relating it to Eliot's use of the same word. I think that Marlow's statement does suggest the sequence of nights and days, but in its own context its immediate and logical meaning is that the light of civilization is but a flicker, a flash, in the abiding darkness that has preceded and must follow. This consideration leads me back to the image and theme of the river, with which *Heart of Darkness* opens and closes. At the opening, Conrad speaks of the service performed by the river: ". . . ages of good service done to the race that peopled its banks . . . The tidal current runs to and fro in its unceasing service . . . It had known and served all the men of whom the nation is proud." Then Marlow imagines the river of Roman times: " 'Sandbanks, marshes, forests, savages . . . death skulking in the air, in the water, in the bush. . . . Land in a swamp, march through the woods, and in some inland post feel the savagery, the utter savagery, had closed round him — all that mysterious life of the wilderness that stirs in the forest, in the jungles, in the hearts of wild men.' " These two accounts, taken together, indicate the ambivalence of the river, of the natural world, and of man. Later in his tale, speaking of the experience of the Europeans in their journey up the African river, and of the savages along its banks, Marlow observes this ambivalence with emphatic directness: " 'We are accustomed to look upon the shackled form of a conquered monster, but there — there you could look at a thing monstrous and free. It was unearthly, and the men were — . . .' "

The idea that the uncivilized is concealed insecurely within civilization is stated here and there in Eliot's writings, both the prose and the poetry. It is explicit particularly in *The Rock*, but it is in *The Dry Salvages*, where river, sea, and ships are dominant images, that the idea appears as a theme that has close parallels with Conrad's story. In the opening lines of this Quartet the river is presented as a symbol of the savagery and destructiveness lurking within civilization and within man:

> I do not know much about gods; but I think that the river
> Is a strong brown god — sullen, untamed and intractable,
> Patient to some degree, at first recognised as a frontier;
> Useful, untrustworthy, as a conveyor of commerce;
> Then only a problem confronting the builder of bridges.
> The problem once solved, the brown god is almost
>     forgotten
> By dwellers in cities — ever, however, implacable,
> Keeping his seasons and rages, destroyer, reminder
> Of what men choose to forget. Unhonoured, unpropitiated
> By worshippers of the machine, but waiting, watching
>     and waiting.
>
> .   .   .   .   .   .   .   .   .   .   .   .   .   .   .
>
> The river is within us, the sea is all about us.

Eliot has assumed here a primitive view of the river as a "strong brown god" in order to suggest the essentially unchanging and limited status of man in relation to the forces of nature and within himself. The mystery and terror of man's plight in time and nature may be obscured by civilization, by instruments and concepts of his own devising, but they reside beneath these as aspects of his own identity — "what men choose to forget." An argument, so to speak, of *The Dry Salvages*, is that man is incapable of seeing his relationship to the supernatural world because he refuses to see his true and unchanging relationship to the natural world. Morally and theologically this may be stated (as Eliot has in effect stated it) as man's inability to believe in the existence of the good (and hence of God) because he refuses to admit and to recognize the existence of evil. Eliot has said of *Heart of Darkness* that it is an eminent instance of the literary evocation of evil,* and we can see how it might be regarded as a representation of the concept of original sin in fresh and secular terms. This consideration is enforced by other correspondences between Eliot and Conrad. The issue is succinctly stated in the second movement of *The Dry Salvages*:

> The backward look behind the assurance
> Of recorded history, the backward half-look
> Over the shoulder, towards the primitive terror.

Exactly such a half-look is taken by Marlow as he speaks of his response to the noisy antics of the savages on the banks of the river:

" 'It was unearthly, and the men were — No, they were not inhuman. . . . Yes, it was ugly enough; but if you were man enough you would admit to yourself that there was in you just the faintest trace of a response to the terrible frankness of that noise, a dim suspicion of there being a meaning in it which you — you so remote from the night of first ages — could comprehend. And why not? The mind of man is capable of anything — because everything is in it, all the past as well as all the future. What was there after all?

---

*Cited by F. O. Matthiessen, *The Achievement of T. S. Eliot* (New York: Oxford, 2nd ed., 1947), p. 24. Matthiessen's reference for the source is not quite clear, but he probably refers to an unpublished lecture which Eliot gave at Harvard in the spring of 1933.

Joy, fear, sorrow, devotion, valor, rage — who can tell? — but truth
— truth stripped of its cloak of time.' "

Marlow relates with somewhat grim humor that he did not " 'go
ashore for a howl and a dance' " because he was too busy repairing
and steering the ship, but he arrives, nonetheless, at a solemn observation: " 'There was surface truth enough in these things to
save a wiser man.' " Just a few paragraphs earlier he has testified
that he glimpsed the deeper truth within himself while he was
engaged in guiding the ship into the weird stillness of the jungle:
" 'One's past came back to one . . . in the shape of an unrestful
and noisy dream.' " But it was only a glimpse. " 'When you have
to attend to things of that sort, to the mere incidents of the surface,
the reality — the reality, I tell you — fades. The inner truth is hidden — luckily, luckily.' " A similar observation is contained in *The
Dry Salvages* where, toward the end of the second movement, Eliot
develops the idea that "the moments of agony" have a kind of
permanence,

> . . . such permanence as time has. We appreciate this better
> In the agony of others, nearly experienced,
> Involving ourselves, than in our own.
> For our own past is covered by the currents of action,
> But the torment of others remains an experience
> Unqualified, unworn by subsequent attrition.

There is here a correspondence of "the currents of action" with
Marlow's "surface truth" — but I would like to suggest that this
passage has a larger relevance to *Heart of Darkness*, to its structure and to its central situation.

Although Marlow as narrator was a habitual device of Conrad,
his function here takes on a special significance in the light of
Eliot's statement. It is the agony of Kurtz, who did "go ashore
for a howl and a dance" and so much else, in which Marlow is
involved, which he appreciated and nearly experienced. While it
was Kurtz who had the vision of horror, it was Marlow who had
the vision of Kurtz and whose fate it was to contemplate and then
to spell out the meaning of the horror. Marlow says, " 'It was his
extremity that I seemed to have lived through,' " and this extrem-

ity, this victorious agony, became for Marlow a permanence, to which he was loyal " 'to the last, and even beyond.' " But the moment of Kurtz's tormented vision is transmuted into permanence not only in Marlow's "appreciation" of it, but also in the achieved art of Conrad's story. The "agony of others" is relayed, so to speak, from the *heart of darkness,* from "the whole universe . . . all the hearts that beat in the darkness" — relayed to Kurtz to Marlow to Conrad to the readers. There is in all this something of deliberate paradox, for both Conrad and Eliot convey a meaning that somehow partakes of the ineffable — a meaning that has its fullness only when the quality of ineffability has been preserved. This is managed ingeniously by Conrad. The story turns upon itself without loss of plausibility when Marlow interrupts his narrative to address his mates directly:

" '. . . He was just a word for me. I did not see the man in the name any more than you do. Do you see him? Do you see the story? Do you see anything? It seems to me I am trying to tell you a dream — making a vain attempt, because no relation of a dream can convey the dream-sensation, that commingling of absurdity, surprise, and bewilderment in a tremor of struggling revolt, that notion of being captured by the incredible which is of the very essence of dreams. . . .

" '. . . No, it is impossible; it is impossible to convey the life-sensation of any given epoch of one's existence — that which makes its truth, its meaning — its subtle and penetrating essence. It is impossible. We live, as we dream — alone. . . .

" 'Of course in this you fellows see more than I could then. You see me, whom you know.' "

In this passage, and finally in the entire story, Conrad illustrates Eliot's insight that "approach to the meaning restores the experience / In a different form" (*The Dry Salvages*). Early in the story Conrad anticipates and points up the question of ineffability by describing the still untold tale as "one of Marlow's inconclusive experiences," and by stating that to Marlow "the meaning of an episode was not inside like a kernel but outside, enveloping the tale which brought it out only as a glow brings out a haze, in the likeness of one of these misty halos that sometimes are made visible by the spectral illumination of moonshine."

## IV

I have been noting that there is a correspondence between Eliot and Conrad in regard to the questions of meaning, truth, reality, and their relationship to time, and there remains something more to be said about this correspondence. I shall pursue the subject by first reviewing, briefly, the theme of ineffability in *Four Quartets* and Eliot's plays. This theme is, indeed, one of those that are explored most persistently throughout *Four Quartets*, where there is a constant return to the interrelated problems of language, experience, and reality. As the theme is stated in *Burnt Norton* — "human kind / Cannot bear very much reality" — it suggests both Conrad's story and Eliot's plays. Specifically, we may remember Marlow's recoil from reality: " 'The inner truth is hidden — luckily, luckily.' " The identical words from *Burnt Norton* are spoken by Thomas to the Women of Canterbury at that "one moment" when they have had their vision of horror, expressed in the Chorus beginning "I have smelt them, the death-bringers," and when Thomas, finally prepared for martyrdom, has had his vision of glory, "a tremor of bliss, a wink of heaven, a whisper." Later, while Thomas' vision is being fulfilled in martyrdom, while he is being murdered, the Women say

> Every horror had its definition,
>
> . . . . . . . . . . .
>
> But this, this is out of life, this is out of time,
> An instant eternity of evil and wrong.

Thus, both Thomas and the Women have glimpsed that reality of which humankind cannot bear very much, for it is the reality that is "out of time" — for the Saint, before his actual martyrdom, it is a tremor, a wink, a whisper of glory, and for the Women it is an "instant eternity" of horror that is beyond definition. Relevant here, as well as more generally, is Eliot's memorable pronouncement: "But the essential advantage for a poet is not, to have a beautiful world with which to deal: it is to be able to see beneath both beauty and ugliness; to see the boredom, and the horror, and the glory" (*The Use of Poetry and the Use of Criticism*). "Beneath both beauty and ugliness" is, of course, the reality that is beneath the surfaces of time and action — or we might better say *realities*, since there are the three levels, coexisting. The boredom is the first step, the first stage, a self-conscious disengagement from the surfaces, a seeing of the surfaces as unreal. To *see* the unreal is boredom, to see the boredom is horror, and to see the horror is glory. I have merely, and hastily, noted some of the implications of Eliot's statement, for my purpose is primarily to cite the statement, since it is necessary to move on.

In *The Family Reunion* it is, of course, Harry who is obsessed with the ineffable. Early in the play he speaks, from his world of horror, to the family:

> You will understand less after I have explained it.
> All that I could hope to make you understand
> Is only events: not what has happened.
> . . . . . . . . . . . . . . . . . .
>
> . . . I tell you, life would be unendurable
> If you were wide awake. You do not know
> The noxious smell untraceable in the drains,
> . . . . . . . . . . . . . . . . . .
>
> . . . As for what happens —
> Of the past, you can only see what is past,
> Not what is always present. That is what matters.
> . . . . . . . . . . . . . . . . . .
>
> This is what matters, but it is unspeakable,
> Untranslatable: I talk in general terms
> Because the particular has no language.

There is here a cluster of familiar elements. The first and last excerpts refer to an ineffable meaning that lies beneath the surface of events. In the middle excerpts there are the unbearable reality; the invisible evil symbolized here and in *Murder in the Cathedral* by smell, the most intimate and obscurest of the senses; and "what is always present . . . what matters," again the ineffable meaning that is beyond time. Toward the end of the play, reconciled to his vision of horror and having chosen the "long journey," Harry says, "I do not know the words in which to explain it." And in his parting speech to the family he says,

I would explain, but you would none of you believe it;
If you believed it, still you would not understand.
You can't know why I'm going. You have not seen
What I have seen.

To maintain the relationship with Conrad, we should recall Marlow's " 'truth stripped of its cloak of time' "; his exclamation that it is impossible to convey one's experience, " 'that which makes its truth, its meaning' "; and his feeling that his fellow Europeans " 'could not possibly know the things I knew.' "

In *The Cocktail Party* and *The Confidential Clerk* the theme of the ineffable is neither so prominent nor so pointed as it is in the earlier plays. This is so, I believe, because the later plays not only are contemporary in their materials but are also an attempt to approach more closely the contemporary experience. I shall soon consider this subject more fully in connection with another matter, and turn now to instances of the ineffable in the plays. Through much of *The Cocktail Party* the ineffable is represented not so much by particular instances or statements as by the relations among the characters (meaning Edward and Lavinia Chamberlayne, Celia Coplestone, and Peter Quilpe), who are all isolated, while struggling to understand themselves and each other. Their alienation, unlike Harry's, is not from a world, but again, from themselves and each other. When we do get overt and immediate references to the ineffable, they are less conspicuous, more continuous with a dramatic context of "ordinary" action than in the earlier plays. There is such a reference toward the end of Act I of *The Cocktail Party*, where Edward and Lavinia are reunited but not yet reconciled with each other.

EDWARD:

There was a door
And I could not open it. I could not touch
the handle.
Why could I not walk out of my prison?
What is hell? Hell is oneself,
Hell is alone, the other figures in it
Merely projections. There is nothing to escape from
And nothing to escape to. One is always alone.

127

LAVINIA:

> Edward, what *are* you talking about?
> Talking to yourself. Could you bear, for a moment,
> To think about *me*?

EDWARD:

>                                          It was only yesterday
> That damnation took place. And now I must
>     live with it
> Day by day, hour by hour, forever and ever.

LAVINIA:

> I think you're on the edge of a nervous
>     breakdown!

Another such reference comes at the end of Act II, but it is not so much an instance as a whole episode — Celia's crucial consultation with the psychiatrist Sir Henry Harcourt-Reilly. Celia, like Edward, is reacting to the collapse of their affair with each other, and she too feels isolated in a personal hell:

> . . . I mean that what has happened has made me aware
> That I've always been alone. That one always is alone.
>
> .  .  .  .  .  .  .  .  .  .  .  .  .  .  .  .  .  .
>
> It no longer seems worth while to *speak* to anyone!

When the doctor describes the condition of

> . . . final desolation
> Of solitude in the phantasmal world
> Of imagination, shuffling memories and desires

Celia says, "That is the hell I have been in." It is probably obvious that the hellish and inarticulate isolation of Edward and Celia is like that of Harry ("one is still alone/ In an over-crowded desert, jostled by ghosts") and of the Women of Canterbury ("emptiness, absence, the Void") and of Marlow during his illness and on his return to the "sepulchral city."

In *The Confidential Clerk* the theme of the ineffable reality is even less intensely suggested than in *The Cocktail Party*. But it is nonetheless to be found. Sir Claude Mulhammer converses with Colby Simpkins as one frustrated artist to another and he speaks of their art, whether music or pottery, as the *other* reality:

. . . it is escape into living,

. . . . . . . . . .

. . . a world where the form is the reality,
Of which the substantial is only a shadow.

. . . . . . . . . . . . . .

And when you are alone at your piano, in the evening,
I believe you will go through the private door
Into the real world, as I do, sometimes.

In another conversation about Colby's frustrated musical career,
Lucasta Angel remarks to him:

But it's only the outer world that you've lost:
You've still got your inner world — a world that's
    more real.
That's why you're different from the rest of us:
You have your secret garden. To which you can retire
And lock the gate behind you.

But nowhere in *The Confidental Clerk* is there a hint of the unbearable reality beyond time.

Before considering further the differences between the earlier
and later plays, I should like to show once more how the theme
of the timeless and unbearable reality corresponds with *Heart of
Darkness*. For this I turn to the end of the story, where Marlow,
more than a year after Kurtz's death, loyally brings to Kurtz's
Intended " 'a slim packet of letters and the girl's portrait.' " In this
episode Conrad consummates a theme that he has been developing
throughout the story: that all times are somehow identical, having
their identity in a reality that binds the present to the past and the
civilized to the uncivilized. This final development of the theme
begins with Marlow calling at the residence of the girl in " 'a street
as still and decorous as a well-kept alley in a cemetery.' " As he
makes his way to the girl's apartment, he has a vision of Kurtz:

" 'He lived then before me; he lived as much as he had ever lived
. . . I rang the bell before a mahogany door on the first floor, and
while I waited he seemed to stare at me out of the glassy panel —
stare with that wide and immense stare embracing, condemning,
loathing all the universe. I seemed to hear the whispered cry, "The
horror! The horror!" ' "

And then, as Marlow meets the girl and shakes hands with her there is a merging of past and present, of death and life, of horror and glory, of light and darkness in a single moment of consciousness:

" '. . . I perceived she was one of those creatures that are not the playthings of Time. For her he had died only yesterday. And, by Jove! the impression was so powerful that for me, too, he seemed to have died only yesterday — nay, this very minute. I saw her and him in the same instant of time — his death and her sorrow — I saw her sorrow in the very moment of his death. Do you understand? I saw them together — I heard them together. She had said, with a deep catch of the breath, "I have survived" while my strained ears seemed to hear distinctly, minged with her tone of despairing regret, the summing-up whisper of his eternal condemnation. I asked myself what I was doing there, with a sensation of panic in my heart as though I had blundered into a place of cruel and absurd mysteries not fit for a human being to behold.' "

This is the ineffable meaning, the hidden truth, the reality in the moment out of time, of which humankind cannot bear very much, and it is the theme that reverberates throughout Eliot's work, the end and the beginning, whether it be "the moment in the rose-garden" or the "instant eternity of evil and wrong."

I shall assume that this matter is already sufficiently illustrated, and that no further citation from Eliot's work is necessary. But I would dwell for a moment on the correspondence of Eliot with Conrad in the paradoxical fusion of opposites. For Marlow the horror of Kurtz has become fused with the glory of the girl. For it is clear that the girl is meant to represent glory, "the heart of light" (Eliot's phrase occurring in the "Hyacinth garden" passage of *The Waste Land* and also in the "rose-garden" passage of *Burnt Norton*). She is described as " 'a soul as translucently pure as a cliff of crystal.' " Marlow sees in her " 'the unextinguishable light of belief and love . . . that great and saving illusion that shone with an unearthly glow in the darkness, in the triumphant darkness.' " ("And the light shineth in darkness, and the darkness comprehended it not"!) The conjunction of glory and horror is suggested again when Marlow, intending to tell the girl a merciful lie, says that Kurtz's last word was her name — again the cruel and absurd mystery of the glory and the horror interpenetrating each other and becoming one. Both Kurtz and the girl become a permanence for Marlow:

" 'I shall see this eloquent phantom as long as I live, and I shall see her, too, a tragic and familiar Shade, resembling in this gesture another one, tragic also, and bedecked with powerless charms, stretching bare brown arms over the glitter of the infernal stream, the stream of darkness.' "

In this passage Conrad gives still another symbolic representation of the theme that the day of the present and of civilization is essentially the same as "the night of first ages." The gesture is that of putting " 'out her arms as if after a retreating figure, stretching them black and with clasped pale hands across the fading and narrow sheen of the window.' " And the other one, " 'tragic also,' " is the African woman, " 'wild and gorgeous,' " who had had Kurtz for lover, and who had appeared on the bank of the river when the dying Kurtz was already aboard the ship that was about to leave. She too, out of the pained frustration of love and grief, had gestured, " 'opened her bared arms and threw them up rigid above her head, as though in an uncontrollable desire to touch the sky.' "
The two women, the white girl and the African, merge to become a type of *la figlia che piange*. In Eliot's poem of that title (that Laforguean poem!) there are images like those of Conrad. The girl who is to weave the sunlight in her hair is like the Intended — " 'her hair seemed to catch all the remaining light in a glimmer of gold.' " And the same girl who is to turn away with a fugitive resentment in her eyes is like the African — " 'She turned away slowly, walked on, following the bank, and passed into the bushes to the left. Once only her eyes gleamed back at us in the dusk of the thickets before she disappeared.' " The last lines of Eliot's poem might be lines for the Marlow who sees all his life the gestures of the composite woman:

And I wonder how they should have been together!
I should have lost a gesture and a pose.
Sometimes these cogitations still amaze
The troubled midnight and the noon's repose.

"How they should have been together," Kurtz and the Intended, Kurtz and the African, and then all of them, everything, the horror and the glory, all incredibly, unbearably, yet irrevocably fused in Marlow's vision and his memory of the vision — this is the amazing question that emerges from Marlow's tale and Conrad's story. " 'Do you understand? I saw them together — I heard them together.' "

### V

There is one matter of correspondence between Eliot and Conrad, and also Laforgue, which I have deferred until the last because there is also involved an apparent development and change in Eliot's attitude. The theme I refer to harks back to those key "Eliotic" passages of Laforgue and Conrad, expressed respectively in each as "les petites gens de l'Histoire" and "commonplace individuals going about their business." In each case there is a protagonist (Hamlet, Marlow) who stands apart from the generality of mankind. An attitude of isolation has commonly been noted in Eliot's work, from the poems of *Prufrock* through *The Waste Land*. In the light of this issue, Eliot may be regarded as sharing with those generations of the late nineteenth and early twentieth centuries the obsession expressed by Pater's injunction to burn with a hard gemlike flame. For Eliot the flame eventually became the flame of religious love, of the Christian and self-sacrificing saint — a figure nonetheless isolated from others. Such a figure we have, of course, in *Murder in the Cathedral*, where Thomas is a type of the saint and the Women are a type of the ordinary people, and the two types are at a polar distance from each other. This relationship is meaningful according to Christian doctrine and tradition, but it is also of the pattern of the individual isolated from society.

It was noted earlier that there is an actual echoing of Laforgue's *petites gens* in *Murder in the Cathedral*. The Women are the *petites gens*, the "small folk," a point re-emphasized at the very end of the play: "we acknowledge ourselves as type of the common man,/ Of the men and women who shut the door and sit by the fire." In *The Family Reunion* there is no such precise echoing of

Laforgue or of Conrad on this score, but the same materials are obviously present. In the earlier part of the play Harry is the individual who, with his vision of the hidden reality, is isolated from society, from the members of his family. And in the latter part, if he does not achieve, at least he approaches the type of the saint. In the climactic scene of recognition and reversal (Part II, Scene ii), his Aunt Agatha says of him

> . . . It is possible
> You are the consciousness of your unhappy family,
> Its bird sent flying through the purgatorial flame.

And at the end of the scene Harry declares his commitment, in a kind of catalogue, to the saintly life:

> To the worship in the desert, the thirst and
>     deprivation,
> A stony sanctuary and a primitive altar,
> The heat of the sun and the icy vigil,
> A care over lives of humble people,
> The lesson of ignorance, of incurable diseases.

Curiously enough, despite their material means and high social position, Harry's family are another kind of humble people, comparable in several respects to the Women of Canterbury — particularly the two aunts and two uncles, who constitute a Chorus in the play. Like the Women, they are but "living and partly living," engrossed in the surfaces of life, unaware of, yet fearing, the deeper and hidden reality. It is at those moments in the play when they speak together as the Chorus that they give such an account of themselves:

> Hold tight, hold tight, we must insist that the world is
>     what we have always taken it to be.
>
> ·  ·  ·  ·  ·  ·  ·  ·  ·  ·  ·  ·  ·  ·
>
> We understand the ordinary business of living,
>
> ·  ·  ·  ·  ·  ·  ·  ·  ·  ·  ·  ·  ·  ·
>
> But the circle of our understanding
> Is a very restricted area.
> Except for a limited number
> Of strictly practical purposes
> We do not know what we are doing . .

Eliot's first two plays show a clear parallelism with each other. In each there is the pattern of isolation from ordinary living found in Laforgue and Conrad. The isolation is spotlighted against the background of ordinary living, the ineffable depths against the known surfaces. The later plays differ in these respects from the earlier. If most of Eliot's work has been an expression of alienation from the world, the last two plays show that the lonely pilgrimage has eventually turned him back toward it. This change, this reconciliation, is implied by Eliot's own criticism of *The Family Reunion*, made in his lecture "Poetry and Drama," given in 1950:

"A more serious evidence [of the play's weaknesses] is that we are left in a divided frame of mind, not knowing whether to consider the play the tragedy of the mother or the salvation of the son. The two situations are not reconciled. I find a confirmation of this in the fact that my sympathies now have come to be all with the mother, who seems to me, except perhaps for the chauffeur, the only complete human being in the play; and my hero now strikes me as an insufferable prig."

This remark has struck me as curious, for I had never doubted Eliot's intention — I had never felt any ambiguity about who was the protagonist in *The Family Reunion*. It was definitely Harry. Eliot still calls him "my hero." Whatever its weaknesses are, the ambiguity is not in the play, but in Eliot's recently developed attitude. Within the framework of the play, Harry is the most complete human being, for he becomes increasingly conscious of the deeper reality, while the mother is only the most forceful person and most fully realized persona in the world of the aunts and uncles, the world of appearances, "what we have always taken it to be . . . the ordinary business of living." Eliot's mentioning the chauffeur is a hyperbole by which emphasis is given to his own newly developed attitude, for the chauffeur has no facet of "completeness," but is merely an ordinary person. He is a stock figure of literary convention, the lowly person and minor character who stands outside the dramatic complication while making a few simple but wise remarks from the sidelines.

The new attitude is, of course, a qualification and partial reversal of the old. Whereas Eliot had for so long divided personal experience and the world at large into the real and the unreal, there is in his latest work a steady drift away from such monism and toward a more traditional dualism. In *The Family Reunion* (in the play itself, not in Eliot's new view of it) there is only one way to reality and it is the way that Harry takes. But in *The Cocktail Party* there are two ways, and

> Neither way is better.
> Both ways are necessary. It is also necessary
> To make a choice between them.

One way, by now familiar in Eliot's work, is the way of the saint, the extraordinary way chosen by Celia Coplestone. The other way is "the common routine . . . casual talk before the fire." (For the context of these phrases see above, in the list of quotations illustrating the Laforgue-Conrad pattern of rhythm, the passage from *The Cocktail Party*.) It is this way, chosen by Edward and Lavinia Chamberlayne, which recalls Laforgue's *petites gens* and Conrad's commonplace individuals, and it recalls also the Women of Canterbury and Harry's aunts and uncles. But not until *The Cocktail Party* (and the later Quartets) is this ordinary way given such sympathetic attention and such emphatic approval. There is a phrase occurring in *The Family Reunion* and in *The Cocktail Party* which, considered in the respective contexts, illustrates nicely the change in attitude that has taken place between the two plays. In the earlier, the aunts and uncles, speaking together as Chorus and in the rhythms recalling *les petites gens*, say

> . . . the transparent deception
> The keeping up of appearances
> The making the best of a bad job
> All twined and tangled together, all are recorded.

In the later play, when it is clear that the Chamberlaynes will be reconciled and that neither will go to the sanitorium, there is this passage:

EDWARD:

> Lavinia, we must make the best of a bad job.
> . . . . . . . . . . . . . . . . .

REILLY:

> When you find, Mr. Chamberlayne,
> The best of a bad job is all any of us make of it —
> Except of course, the saints — such as those who go
> To the sanitorium — you will forget this phrase,
> And in forgetting it will alter the condition.

The recurring phrase has a somewhat different meaning in each case. In the first there is irony and distaste, in the second there is sympathy, approval, and hopefulness. In *The Cocktail Party* there is no ambiguity of the kind Eliot attributes to *The Family Reunion*, but there is a kind of dualism, of the ordinary and extraordinary ways, and it is the ordinary — making the best of a bad job — that is the embracing subject and that is in the foreground of the play.

*The Confidential Clerk* shows a still further development of the new attitude. This may be indicated by making comparisons among the plays. After the religious pageant of St. Thomas, all of them have contemporary settings. In the first of these there is the haunted hero isolated, to the technical detriment of the play, from the other characters. In the next there are the four people, Edward and Lavinia Chamberlayne, Celia Coplestone, and Peter Quilpe, whose fates are more or less manipulated by those quasi-supernatural busybodies, Julia, Alex, and Dr. Harcourt-Reilly. But in the last, whatever its implausibilities, there is a greater realism of character and of character relationship. There are, so to speak, no flat characters, none who are merely dramatic props, such as the aunts and uncles in *The Family Reunion*, Julia and Alex in *The Cocktail Party*. No character in *The Confidential Clerk* is merely dramatic machinery. The characters are different people, not symbols of different categories of reality. Whereas in *The Cocktail Party* two approaches to reality, two ways of living, are distinguished and defined, *The Confidential Clerk* shows a concern for reconciling and integrating the two aspects of reality. In their first long dialogue, when Sir Claude and Colby are discussing their arts, pottery and music, which evoke for them a special reality, Sir Claude remarks that the art in each case, like his wife's occult investigations, is "a kind of substitute for religion." And he adds,

I dare say truly religious people —
I've never known any — can find some unity.
Then there are also the men of genius.
There are others, it seems to me, who have at
    best to live
In two worlds — each a kind of make-believe.
That's you and me.

The two worlds or two realities are not opposites (*The Family Reunion*) or alternatives (*The Cocktail Party*) but complementary. This theme is represented in *The Confidential Clerk* by a symbolic image that is familiar and recurrent in Eliot's work. Very early in the play, when Eggerson and Sir Claude are discussing Colby's living quarters, Eggerson makes a suggestion:

He's expressed such an interest in my garden
That I think he ought to have window boxes.
Some day he'll want a garden of his own.

Later, when Lucasta tells Colby that he has a garden where there are music and flowers that are exclusively his own, he answers that this garden and the ordinary world are equally real in being equally unreal —

. . . that's just the trouble. They seem so unrelated.
I turn the key and walk through the gate,
And there I am . . . alone, in my 'garden.'
Alone, that's the thing. That's why it's not real.
You know, I think that Eggerson's garden
Is more real than mine.

. . . . . . . .

. . . he retires to his garden — literally,
And also in the same sense that I retire to mine.
But he doesn't feel alone there. And when he
    comes out
He has marrows, or beetroot, or peas . . . for
    Mrs. Eggerson.

. . . . . . . . . . . .

What I mean is, my garden's no less unreal to me
Than the world outside it. If you have two lives
Which have nothing whatever to do with each
    other —

Well, they're both unreal. But for Eggerson
His garden is part of one single world.

. . . . . . . . . . . .

If I were religious, God would walk in my garden
And that would make the world outside it real
And acceptable, I think.

The mystical, or at least metaphysically symbolic, rose-garden has
given way to, or been merged with, the actual vegetable garden —
Eggerson's garden. At the end of the play it is Eggerson who in-
forms Colby that he (Colby) is religious and who predicts for him
a vocation in the church. As for Eggerson himself, it turns out
that he is the Vicar's Warden and has always been a Christian,
despite Sir Claude's remark earlier that he has never known any
truly religious people, although he has known Eggerson for practically a lifetime. While the other characters — Sir Claude, Lady
Elizabeth, and Mrs. Guzzard — struggle and compete with each
other for a son — for Colby — it is Eggerson, also in need of a son,
who effortlessly wins him for his own home and as church organist
in his parish of Joshua Park. (There may be a deliberate significance in that name, for Joshua — *Yehoshua* — is the Hebrew of
which the Hellenized form is Jesus. Hence, Jesus Park: God in
the garden.) Colby is in some ways the same type of Eliotic character as Thomas, Harry, and Celia Coplestone, and yet, significantly,
he is not a type of the saint. Both Colby and Eggerson are confidential clerks, but it is a mild irony of the play that it is Eggerson
who is *the* confidential (trusting, believing) clerk, the humble hero
of the play, for Eggerson is one of *les petites gens*, a commonplace
Christian, both ordinary and extraordinary at once.

There is one more point of difference between the plays that
seems worth making here. In *The Cocktail Party* the doctor's description to Celia of the "common routine," though he calls it "a
good life," is really somewhat depressing. He pictures man and
wife as

Two people who know they do not understand each other,
Breeding children whom they do not understand
And who will never understand them.

In this statement the common lot — the relation of husband and wife, of parent and child, of person and person — is viewed as one static condition which is the negation of another static condition, understanding. It is as if understanding, in this reference, were an ultimate insight, a contemplation once and for all of an abiding truth. Behind this use of the word *understand* is the idea of the essential reality which, by definition, is the object requiring such ultimate understanding, so that this use of it, with reference to human relationships, is somewhat irrelevant. The question of understanding is raised again in *The Confidential Clerk* as if to correct or to qualify the statement of the earlier play. In their long intimate dialogue, Colby tells Lucasta:

> I meant, there's no end to understanding a person.
> All one can do is to understand them better,
> To keep up with them; so that as the other changes
> You can understand the change as soon as it happens,
> Though you couldn't have predicted it.

And the play ends precisely on the question of understanding between parents and children. Lady Elizabeth says, "Claude, we've got to try to understand our children." And Kaghan, speaking of himself and his future wife, Lucasta, says, "And we should like to understand *you*."

After *The Family Reunion* Eliot's plays show a waning emphasis on the isolated individual and the ineffable reality, and a growing interest in the common lot and the ordinary reality. It may be noted, for whatever it is worth, that the later plays show an increasing unity of situation and of action but diminish steadily in the intensity of poetic language.

Change of attitude is less prominent in *Four Quartets* than in the plays, and there are probable explanations why this is so. For one thing, the poem is a single work under a single title. *Four Quartets* was, moreover, composed within a briefer span of time than the plays. A listing of publication dates is significant here: *Burnt Norton*, 1935; *Murder in the Cathedral*, 1935; *The Family Reunion*, 1939; *East Coker*, 1940; *The Dry Salvages*, 1941; *Little Gidding*, 1942; *Four Quartets*, 1943; *The Cocktail Party*, 1949;

*The Confidential Clerk,* 1953. It is to be noted that there is a considerable time span between *Burnt Norton* and *East Coker,* that *The Family Reunion* was written before *East Coker,* and that the last three Quartets were written in relatively quick succession. Conceivably Eliot planned *Four Quartets* as a single work only some time after he had written *Burnt Norton,* which was published as an individual poem in the book *Collected Poems 1909–1935.* If this is so, it is consistent with Eliot's frequent practice of making a new composition have a retroactive effect upon his earlier work, and with his statements to the effect that each of a writer's compositions has, besides its own unity, a place in the larger unity of his entire work. *Four Quartets* has, indeed, this kind of ambiguity, for its title is that of a single work and yet collective in its meaning.

But to return to the change of attitude, it is most marked between *Burnt Norton* on the one hand and the later pieces on the other. Compared with the other Quartets, *Burnt Norton* is in greater degree abstract and personal, more steadily preoccupied with the discontinuity between reality and the temporal world — "To be conscious is not to be in time." Such references as are made to the world, to people, are in the mood of alienation — for example, "the strained time-ridden faces" and "The loud lament of the disconsolate chimera." But the other Quartets abound with references, and sympathetic references, to the life of the external world. In *East Coker* there are the people of Sir Thomas Elyot's sixteenth-century England, "The association of man and woman." In *The Dry Salvages* there are the "anxious worried women." And in *Little Gidding* there is the concern with history and England. Whereas *Burnt Norton* is preoccupied with the quest for the personal experience of the moment out of time —

> Ridiculous the waste sad time
> Stretching before and after —

in *The Dry Salvages* it is stated that

> . . . right action is freedom
> From past and future also.
> For most of us, this is the aim

Never here to be realised;
Who are only undefeated
Because we have gone on trying.

All of the Quartets are personal, but a difference may be indicated
by calling *Burnt Norton private* and the others *intimate*. Eliot has
himself made a distinction, in "The Three Voices of Poetry"
(1953), which is applicable here. "The first is the voice of the poet
talking to himself — or to nobody. The second is the voice of the
poet addressing an audience, whether large or small."

In the later Quartets the second voice is relatively stronger and
more frequent. Change of attitude is not only generally implicit in
the later Quartets but is also an immediate subject — as in *East
Coker*:

. . . one has only learnt to get the better of words
For the thing one no longer has to say, or the way
  in which
One is no longer disposed to say it.

The change of attitude may be accounted for by what we call
simply, and vaguely, development, and also, of course, by Eliot's
continuing commitment to Christian belief. But it is to be noted
that the change first appears, is first announced, in *East Coker*, the
first of the later Quartets, all of which were written during World
War II. An obvious inference is that the change was produced by
the impact of the war. In these Quartets, there is a steady increase
in reference to the war, a progressive integration of that subject
with Eliot's enduring themes — an adjustment of the themes to the
subject. In *Four Quartets* the second voice intends to speak not
only to an audience, but for an audience, for a people in the circumstantial plight of war, and also for people in the universal
plight of living, for "les petites gens de l'Histoire" and for "commonplace individuals going about their business." The change of
attitude in the later Quartets and the later plays was not so much
a change in principles as in mood. The position remained the
same while the perspective was extended and broadened. It was
not the identity but the identification that had changed.

My subject has been the relationship of Eliot's poetry to La-

forgue's "Hamlet" and especially to Conrad's *Heart of Darkness.*
If there is something of the miscellaneous about my discussion, I
hope that this quality, besides being a limitation, is also a valid
comment on the complexity of the subject. The complexity of
Eliot's literary relationships exists, of course, with respect not only
to one or two writers, but to many. There are places in Eliot's
work, and general aspects of his work, for which I have offered
Conrad as, so to speak, a source, but for which other writers could
equally be claimed — Dante, St. John of the Cross, Baudelaire, for
example, and perhaps still others. It is characteristic of Eliot to
echo not only an individual source, but whole congeries of sources
at once. We have seen that there are certain ideas and a particular
pattern of rhythm which Eliot took neither from Laforgue nor
Conrad, alone, but from both — or did he take them from the
Bible?

A familiar theme of Eliot's criticism, since "Tradition and the
Individual Talent," has been the use which one writer makes of
others, particularly of his predecessors. In that early essay he said,
with regard to the poet, that "not only the best, but the most
individual parts of his work may be those in which the dead poets,
his ancestors, assert their immortality most vigorously." He also
said that it is not "preposterous that the past should be altered by
the present as much as the present is directed by the past." Although Conrad was not strictly a poet, and although he was still
alive when his earlier prose first began to affect Eliot's poetry, these
remarks are true about the relationship of the two writers. There
are qualities in each which are enhanced, which emerge with
greater fullness and clarity in the light of the relationship. Each
writer nourishes and augments the other without a loss resulting
in either quarter. The remarkable thing, the thing that is not, after
all, "preposterous" is that the earlier writer should be "altered"
by the later. For has not Eliot's use of Conrad's story probed new
depths of its meaning and shown new virtues of its thematic form?
It is not that Eliot has imposed any meaning or form on Conrad,
but that he has uncovered (and in that sense, altered) what was
already there. If this is so, it illustrates a singular virtue of Eliot's

work. Since Ben Jonson — indeed, since Horace — there has been conscious theorizing about the writer's use of other writers, and the principle of influence has provided seemingly endless tasks for modern scholarship. But no writer has illustrated the fact of influence so forcefully, so variously, and so dramatically as Eliot has. There is a respect in which Eliot's eminence as a critic is better documented by his poetry than by his prose. A diligent reading of Eliot's poetry becomes often a diligent reading of his sources and brings a new perspective on the sources. He said in the essay, "No poet, no artist of any art, has his complete meaning alone" — and as he takes us among other writers to complete his own meaning, he makes their meaning more complete also. Like the successful critic, he teaches us to share his ability to read. He leads us, as Virgil led Dante, not only into regions previously unknown, but also to a fuller understanding and a deeper appreciation of what was already familiar.

## AFTER-NOTES*

By "the earlier Conrad" Eliot meant, I believe, other works as well as *Heart of Darkness*, but it was this story which evidently made the deepest and most influential impression upon him. Although not specified as such, it is obviously the earlier Conrad, and especially *Heart of Darkness*, that Eliot characterized when, in 1919, he gave Conrad the highest praise, while contrasting him with Kipling:

". . . some poets, like Shakespeare or Dante or Villon, and some novelists, like Mr. Conrad, have, in contrast to ideas or concepts, points of view, or 'worlds' — what are incorrectly called 'philosophies.' Mr. Conrad is very germane to the question, because he is in many ways the antithesis of Mr. Kipling. He is, for one thing, the antithesis of Empire (as well as democracy); his characters are the denial of Empire, of Nation, of Race almost, they are fearfully alone with the Wilderness. Mr. Conrad has no ideas, but he

*The titles and publication dates of Conrad's works referred to here are as follows: *An Outcast of the Islands*, 1896; "An Outpost of Progress" and "The Return," contained in *Tales of Unrest*, 1898; *Lord Jim*, 1900; *Youth* and *Heart of Darkness*, contained in *Youth*, 1902; "Amy Foster," contained in *Typhoon and Other Stories*, 1903; *The Shadow-Line*, 1917.

has a point of view, a 'world'; it can hardly be defined, but it pervades his work and is unmistakable." *

While it may be hard to define the "world" that pervades all of Conrad's work, the theme of man "fearfully alone with the Wilderness" is certainly most pervasive and predominant in the earlier novels and stories, and it is represented most vividly and definitively by *Heart of Darkness*.

In my deliberate reading of Conrad's earlier fiction I have found nothing comparable to *Heart of Darkness* for extensive and complex relationship with Eliot's poetry. The experience of reading did, however, clarify Eliot's reference to the earlier Conrad in general rather than to the particular story. In this earlier fiction, even when there are no precise sources, if one anticipates a relationship with, a suggestion of, Eliot, one finds it in the quality of the effect produced by Conrad's subject and meaning and style. One finds recurrently in Conrad what Eliot called, in the essay on Swinburne, "Language . . . so close to the object that the two are identified," and Conrad's "objects" are often like those rendered by Eliot's language, too. This proposition cannot be readily demonstrated, and I am not inclined to amass a copious body of excerpts from Conrad to urge so elusive and tenuous a point, although I believe that the point is actually valid. But I shall quote here a characteristic passage which bears on it. It is a comment by Marlow, in *Lord Jim*, on Jim's predicament in the remoteness of Patusan:

" 'I suppose I must have fallen into a sentimental mood; I only know that I stood there long enough for the sense of utter solitude to get hold of me so completely that all I had lately seen, all I had heard, and the very human speech itself, seemed to have passed away out of existence, living only for a while longer in my memory, as though I had been the last of mankind. It was a strange and melancholy illusion, evolved half-consciously like all our illusions, which I suspect only to be visions of remote unattainable truth, seen dimly. This was, indeed, one of the lost, forgotten, unknown places of the earth; I had looked under its obscure surface, and I

---

* "Kipling Redivivus," *Athenaeum*, May 9, 1919, pp. 297–298. This is a review of Kipling's volume of poems *The Years Between*.

felt that when to-morrow I had left it forever, it would slip out of existence, to live only in my memory till I myself passed into oblivion. I have that feeling about me now; perhaps it is that feeling which had incited me to tell you the story, to try to hand over to you, as it were, its very existence, its reality — the truth disclosed in a moment of illusion.' "

This passage is like many others with which Conrad or Marlow or some other narrator intrudes, so to speak, upon the story in order to probe its meaning — not to give a judgment or an opinion or an explanation, but to suggest briefly, intensely, dramatically "that feeling" which is an essential part of a meaning — "its very existence, its reality" — a meaning, it appears, not otherwise translatable. Common to this passage and others is that truth which lies beneath the surface, and also the word *illusion* which, as Conrad uses it, is centrally relevant to his intellectual and emotional outlook. This subject — or "object" — so frequent in Conrad's work, is equally frequent in Eliot's. There are in Eliot's poetry many "moments" — the moment of consciousness, the moment of distraction, the moment of vision — which are comparable to Conrad's "moment of illusion." Conrad's language in such passages as this one shows a psychological impressionism and a dramatic mode of evocation, both of which are also to be found in Eliot's poetry.

As stated above, no single passage is a wholly adequate illustration of those recurring effects in Conrad's writing which, in their cumulative aspect, justify Eliot's praise and at the same time suggest Eliot's poetry. The passage I have quoted is but one among a variety of examples. There are other passages where the object rendered is not an inner experience but an external atmosphere or situation.

In addition to such passages of only general relevance between the two writers, I have, in my reading of Conrad, also come upon a number of actual passages echoed by Eliot's poetry. These I excluded from my essay because Eliot's relation with *Heart of Darkness* appeared sufficiently complex and has its own discrete unity. Before offering these sources and echoes I should say that I am aware of the possibility of having become oversensitized by my preoccupation, of having "found" too readily what I was quite consciously looking for.

1. "An Outpost of Progress" is a shorter and simpler story than *Heart of Darkness*, but it is similar in theme and is also about the ivory trade in Africa. Here, too, Conrad is concerned with the impact of primitive savagery upon the civilized, and with that forbidding reality of human existence which lies beneath both savagery and civilization:

"Few men realize that their life, the very essence of their character, their capabilities and their audacities are only the expression of their belief in the safety of their surroundings. . . . But the contact with pure unmitigated savagery, with primitive nature and primitive man, brings sudden and profound trouble into the heart. To the sentiment of being alone of one's kind, to the clear perception of the loneliness of one's thoughts, of one's sensations — to the negation of the habitual, which is safe, there is added the affirmation of the unusual, which is dangerous; a suggestion of things vague, uncontrollable, and repulsive, whose discomposing intrusion excites the imagination and tries the civilized nerves of the foolish and the wise alike."

This theme of the familiar and the usual is applied with ironical parallelism to both Europeans and Africans. In a single paragraph Conrad comments respectively on Kayerts and Carlier, the two white men at the trading outpost:

"Kayerts . . . regretted the streets, the pavements, the cafés, his friends of many years; all the things he used to see, day after day; all the thoughts suggested by familiar things — the thoughts effortless, monotonous and soothing of a government clerk; he regretted all the gossip, the small enmities, the mild venom, and the little jokes of government offices. . . . [Carlier] regretted the clink of saber and spurs on a fine afternoon, the barrack-room witticisms, the girls of garrison towns."

Later in the story there is this comment on the black workers at the outpost, who are languishing in exile from their own tribe, which is in a remote part of Africa:

"They were not happy, regretting the festive incantations, the sorceries, the human sacrifices of their own land; where they also had parents, brothers, sisters, admired chiefs, respected magicians, loved friends, and other ties supposed generally to be human."

These passages, conspicuous for their combination of similarity and contrast and for the resulting irony, are, I believe, echoed by Eliot in his poem, "Journey of the Magi":

> There were times we regretted
> The summer palaces on slopes, the terraces,
> And the silken girls bringing sherbet.

Eliot's poem has otherwise no significant relation to Conrad's story. But the passage quoted here is strikingly similar to those of Conrad. Both writers use the word *regret* with its meaning of "miss poignantly," and in each case the word is followed by an appropriate and comparable series of references.

Toward the end of the story, when Kayerts and Carlier are both suffering from the effects of their prolonged isolation, they squabble over a trifling matter of rations, soon become violent, and Kayerts fatally shoots Carlier. In Conrad's dramatic account of Kayert's mental response to the predicament there is this passage:

"Then he tried to imagine himself dead, and Carlier sitting in his chair watching him; and his attempt met with such unexpected success, that in a few moments he became not at all sure who was dead and who was alive. This extraordinary achievement of his fancy startled him, however, and by a clever and timely effort of mind he saved himself just in time from becoming Carlier."

I find this passage — especially the expression "who was dead and who was alive" — echoed by Eliot in the second "Fragment" of *Sweeney Agonistes*. Sweeney has been telling his companions of a man who "once did a girl in."

> He didn't know if he was alive
>                     and the girl was dead
> He didn't know if the girl was alive
>                     and he was dead
> He didn't know if they both were alive
>                     or both were dead
> If he was alive then the milkman wasn't
>                     and the rent collector wasn't
> And if they were alive then he was dead.

Conrad's story, both in its comment and in its action, is concerned with the reality that lies beneath ordinary awareness, and Sweeney's account of the man who "did a girl in" implies, for all its absurd grotesqueness, the same subject. Sweeney's man, like Kayerts, is estranged by his evil deed from the ordinary world, the world of the milkman and the rent-collector. Relevant here is Eliot's Baudelairean concept that the experience of evil, even the conscious practice of evil, has a positive value, as compared to the amoral attitude, in that it affirms the existence of an absolute morality.

2. In Conrad's second novel, *An Outcast of the Islands*, there is a passage which is a highly plausible source of some lines in "What the Thunder Said," the last section of *The Waste Land*. The passage comes at that point in the novel when Willems, the outcast, is abandoned by Lingard, the benefactor whom he betrayed — abandoned as a kind of prisoner in the jungle remoteness of a Malayan island. I italicize words and phrases for reference.

". . . Only his eyes seemed to live, as they followed the canoe on its course that carried it away from him, steadily, unhesitatingly, finally, as if it were going not up the great river into the momentous excitement of Sambir, but straight into the past, into the *past* crowded yet *empty*, like an old cemetery full of *neglected graves*, where lie dead hopes that never return.

"From time to time he felt on his face the passing warm touch of an immense breath coming from beyond the forest, like the short panting of an oppressed world. Then the heavy air round him was pierced by a sharp *gust* of wind, *bringing* with it the fresh, *damp* feel of the falling *rain*; and all the innumerable tree-tops of the forests swayed to the left and sprang back again in a tumultuous balancing of nodding branches and shuddering leaves. A light frown ran over the river, the *clouds stirred* slowly, changing their aspect but not their place, as if they had turned ponderously over; and when the sudden movement had died out in a quickened tremor of the slenderest twigs, there was *a short period of formidable immobility* above and below, during which the *voice of the thunder* was heard, *speaking* in a sustained, emphatic and vibrating roll, with violent louder bursts of crashing sound, like a wrathful and threatening *discourse of an angry god*."

Here are Eliot's lines:

> In this decayed hole among the mountains
> In the faint moonlight, the grass is singing
> Over the tumbled graves, about the chapel
> There is the empty chapel, only the wind's home.
> It has no windows, and the door swings,
> Dry bones can harm no one.
> Only a cock stood on the rooftree
> Co co rico co co rico
> In a flash of lightning. Then a damp gust
> Bringing rain
>
> Ganga was sunken, and the limp leaves
> Waited for rain, while the black clouds
> Gathered far distant, over Himavant.
> The jungle crouched, humped in silence.
> Then spoke the thunder
> DA

The similarities are most obvious in the latter parts of the two passages where, in each case, there is description of a storm. Any two descriptions of the same kind of storm will inevitably make a number of similar references and thus probably use even the same words. But the similarities here are compelling beyond such plausible coincidence. In the context of the Conrad-Eliot relationship, Eliot's "damp gust/ Bringing rain" is surely suggested by Conrad's use of precisely the same words in close proximity. This kind of evidence is enough to provoke a search for other signs — and they are discovered. Eliot's "the black clouds/ Gathered" corresponds with Conrad's clouds which "stirred slowly, changing their aspect." Having warmed to the issue, do we not feel a resonance between Eliot's next image — "The jungle crouched, humped in silence" — and Conrad's tree-tops which "swayed . . . and sprang back again," and also with the atmospheric condition preceding the thunder, "a short period of formidable immobility"? And the two passages end with an emphatic correspondence: "the voice of the thunder . . . speaking . . . discourse of an angry god" — "DA. *Datta . . . Dayadhvam . . . Damyata.*" In addition to these details, which are in closely parallel sequences, it may be noted that both storms are in eastern jungles.

If we are persuaded that Eliot's verses echo, in condensed form, Conrad's description of the oncoming storm, we may allow that there are also some correspondences between the earlier parts of both passages — although here the relationships are not nearly so immediate. The most striking similarity is that of Eliot's "tumbled graves" and Conrad's "neglected graves." Eliot's "empty chapel" is surely symbolic, among other things, of the past, and is in this respect equivalent to Conrad's "past crowded yet empty . . . where lie dead hopes that never return." These correspondences might seem forced if they were not actually reinforced by the context and by the impressive sequential parallelism between the details in the entire passages of both writers.

The inherent qualities of Conrad's passage — the language so close to its object — are enough to explain Eliot's use of it, but there are also supporting reasons why Eliot should have been impressed by this scene of Conrad's novel and should have used it where he did in *The Waste Land.* Willem's plight of being isolated in a savage wilderness, cut off from civilization, readily recalls similar plights of characters in *Heart of Darkness* and "An Outpost of Progress." The remainder of Conrad's paragraph about the storm, a bit less than a single page of the novel, is truly one of the most water-laden passages that has ever been written, and the word *water* itself occurs in it eleven times. It should be recalled in this connection that "What the Thunder Said" opens with a passage containing a reference to "thunder of spring over distant mountains." The passage following, lines 331 through 358, beginning "Here is no water but only rock," is the memorable description of the absence of water, vividly evocative of both dryness and its opposite. Curiously enough, the word *water* occurs precisely eleven times in the twenty-eight lines! The exact numerical equation is, of course, of no significance whatsoever. (My desire to convey the nature of Conrad's prose without actually quoting it led me into this counting of words.) But the collocation of all these materials in Conrad and in Eliot is significant. In writing the watery-waterless passage with its "dry sterile thunder without rain," Eliot's preoccupations could have recalled to him Conrad's thunderous storm which produced "heavy big drops . . . with sonorous and rapid beats upon the dry earth" — "Drip drop drip drop drop drop drop." Or Conrad's storm could have already been within the focus of Eliot's imagination, already assimilated into Eliot's impulses and purposes. In any event, there is a rich pattern of correspondences between the final pages of Part IV, Chapter Four, of Conrad's novel and the last section of Eliot's poem.

3. Eliot's symbolic imagery of the rose-garden is certainly traditional and archetypal, and yet it is known that some of the passages in which this imagery appears derive details and qualities from particular sources. These sources are D. H. Lawrence's story "The Shadow in the Rose Garden," the opening pages of *Alice in Wonderland*, where Alice is at first too big to get through the little door beyond which there is a lovely garden, and Kipling's story "They," where there is a preternatural circumstance of children's laughter in the shrubbery.* To this multiplicity of sources may also be added the opening sentences of Conrad's novel *The Shadow-Line*:

"Only the young have such moments. I don't mean the very young. No. The very young have, properly speaking, no moments. It is the privilege of early youth to live in advance of its days in the beautiful continuity of hope which knows no pauses and no introspection.

"One closes behind one the little gate of mere boyishness — and enters an enchanted garden. Its very shades glow with promise. Every turn of the path has its seduction. And it isn't because it is an undiscovered country. One knows well enough that all mankind had streamed that way. It is the charm of universal experience from which one expects an uncommon or personal sensation — a bit of one's own.

"One goes on recognising the landmarks of the predecessors, excited, amused, taking the hard luck and the good luck together — the kicks and the halfpence, as the saying is — the picturesque

---

*See Louis L. Martz, "The Wheel and the Point," in my *T. S. Eliot: A Selected Critique* (New York: Rinehart, 1948); also Helen Gardner, *The Art of T. S. Eliot* (New York: Dutton, 1950), p. 160.

common lot that holds so many possibilities for the deserving or
perhaps for the lucky. Yes. One goes on. And the time, too, goes
on, till one perceives ahead a shadow-line warning one that the
region of early youth, too, must be left behind.

"This is the period of life in which such moments of which I
have spoken are likely to come. What moments? Why the moments
of boredom, of weariness, of dissatisfaction."

All the sources, including this one of Conrad, are most clearly
in evidence in the first section of *Burnt Norton* and in the climactic dialogue of Harry and Agatha in *The Family Reunion*.
I should like to indicate first those elements in Eliot's poetry which
have correspondences in Conrad's prose as well as in some of the
other sources. The most obvious and inclusive material, the common ground, is of course the garden itself. In Eliot there are the
"passage" and the "alley" (*Burnt Norton*), like Conrad's "path";
"the door . . . / Into the rose-garden," "the first gate" (*Burnt
Norton*) and "the little door" (*The Family Reunion*), like Conrad's "little gate"; "a cloud passed" (*Burnt Norton*) and "a black
raven flew over" (*The Family Reunion*), like Conrad's "shadow-
line."

I shall indicate next those elements of Eliot's poetry which cor-
respond more immediately with Conrad than with any of the other
sources. The most explicit correspondence in any of the sources
with "Through the first gate, / Into our first world" of *Burnt
Norton* is Conrad's "little gate of mere boyishness" and also his
"region of early youth." It is in Conrad, as in Eliot, that the garden
and allied details are used in a clearly symbolic rather than in
a circumstantial or allegorical fashion. Eliot's use of first-person
plural pronouns and possessives — "the passage which *we* did not
take," "the door *we* never opened," "*our* first world" — accords
with Conrad's "*all mankind* had streamed that way . . . the
charm of *universal* experience" and "*one* perceives ahead a
shadow-line warning *one*." The Conrad source underscores, and
may even partially explicate, Eliot's symbolization of the universal
experience of early youth and the passing of early youth. Both
passages are discourses on time. Toward the end of the second

section of *Burnt Norton* there is "the moment in the rose-garden," and the word *moments,* used with the same quality of meaning, occurs repeatedly in Conrad's passage. The word *moment* is, indeed, of central and singular importance in Eliot's poetic vocabulary. *The Shadow-Line* (1917) is no longer "the earlier Conrad," and after the opening paragraphs there is nothing in it that is suggestive of the Conrad-Eliot relationship.

4. This final note will treat a number of points of relationship between Eliot and Conrad. None of them is so extensive as those already given, and they vary in character among themselves. Any of them could be mere coincidence. On the other hand, there may very well be points of relationship which I have failed to recognize. But the points presented here, as an accumulation, and within the larger context of the subject, are ultimately relevant.

I had known for some time that the phrase "a handful of dust," in the first section of *The Waste Land,* appears also in John Donne's *Meditations* IV: "What's become of man's great extent and proportion when himself shrinks himself and consumes himself to a handful of dust?" I had vaguely surmised that the phrase came from the Bible. After I had found this same phrase — not once, but twice — in Conrad, I consulted Bible concordances and other appropriate dictionaries, but with negative results. The thirteenth edition of *Bartlett's Familiar Quotations* (1955) contains the phrase in its index, but the only reference is to the lines from *The Waste Land,* quoted in its section on Eliot. (But I still feel that the phrase may have some ultimate source — it is that kind of phrase.) I shall consider first the occurrence in Conrad's story "The Return." The story opens with an account of the desperate and agonized thoughts of a successful English businessman who, on returning home in the evening, finds a note from his wife saying that she has deserted him for another man. This account contains the sentence, "He was afraid with that penetrating faltering fear that seems, in the very middle of a beat, to turn one's heart into a handful of dust." The subject, fear, in addition to the phrase, suggests that it is this statement that is being echoed in Eliot's line, "I will show you fear in a handful of dust." ("The Return," a story concerned with the crisis of moral and spiritual awakening, is otherwise suggestive at several points of likely echoings in *The Waste Land*, as indicated by R. L. Morris, "Eliot's 'Game of Chess' and Conrad's 'The Return,'" *Modern Language Notes*, LXV, 6.) And yet, recalling Eliot's practice of combining multiple sources in a single reference or echo, we should also consider this passage from Conrad's story *Youth*:

". . .'I remember my youth and the feeling that will never come back any more — the feeling that I could last forever, outlast the sea, the earth, and all men; the deceitful feeling that lures us on to joys, to perils, to love, to vain effort — to death; the triumphant conviction of strength, the heat of life in the handful of dust, the glow in the heart that with every year grows dim, grows cold, grows small, and expires — and expires, too soon, too soon, before life itself.'"

There are a number of possible explanations why this phrase should occur in the three writers. There may be some common source of which I am unaware, or there may have been a multiple coincidence — or other possibilities between these extremes. The most attractive explanation for the course of this discussion is that Eliot, having come upon the phrase once in Donne and twice in Conrad, was sufficiently impressed by it to use it in his own poem. That Eliot had read Donne's *Meditations* is beyond question, and that he had read Conrad's stories is more than likely. "The Return" appeared in the volume *Tales of Unrest*, which also contains "An Outpost of Progress," and *Youth* is the title story of the volume containing *Heart of Darkness*.

There are further reasons why the passage from *Youth* is interesting here. The style is strikingly marked by that rhythm — produced by the repetition of words and constructions — which is pervasive in Eliot's verse and intrinsic to the Bible. An appropriate biblical example, and a favorite of Eliot's, would be the opening verses of Ecclesiastes 12, beginning "Remember now thy Creator in the days of thy youth, while the evil days come not," and ending "Then shall the dust return to the earth as it was: and the spirit shall return unto God who gave it." The passage from *Youth*, like some other points of relationship or parallelism between Eliot and Conrad, has the same import as the verses from Ecclesiastes — the vicissitudes of life and the stages of human decay that follow with the passing of time. Another such passage is the one in *The Shadow-Line*, and the two are, I think, of a kind to be readily associated. I say this by way of introducing some lines from Eliot which have, for me, also entered into the association. They are from the description of old age in *Little Gidding*.

> Let me disclose the gifts reserved for age
>> To set a crown upon your lifetime's effort.
>> First, the cold friction of expiring sense
> Without enchantment, offering no promise
>> But bitter tastelessness of shadow fruit
>> As body and soul begin to fall asunder.
> Second, the conscious impotence of rage
>> At human folly, and the laceration
>> Of laughter at what ceases to amuse.
> And last, the rending pain of re-enactment
>> Of all that you have done, and been; the shame
>> Of motives late revealed, and the awareness
> Of things ill done and done to other's harm
>> Which once you took for exercise of virtue.

In Eliot's lines there are similarities to Conrad's prose in diction as well as in meaning. Eliot's words *cold* and *expiring* have equivalents in *Youth*, and the words *enchantment, promise*, and *shadow* have them in *The Shadow-Line*. Eliot's verses give not only a painful picture of waning vitality but also of the vanities and delusions which attend the period of greatest vitality, and the same ambivalence is present in *Youth*. In both passages, Conrad's and Eliot's, there is reference to an awareness which survives the death of other faculties and which, before the end of life, sits in exacting judgment on the life that has been lived.

I have offered these considerations not primarily to suggest that Eliot, in the second section of *Little Gidding*, is echoing Conrad, but rather to indicate further the range of likeness between the two writers — of likeness even when no specific echoing is necessarily involved. I shall end these notes with one more point relevant to this issue, a point of verbal parallelism between the first section of *Little Gidding* and Conrad's "Amy Foster." I refer to these passages:

> And what the dead had no speech for, when living,
> They can tell you being dead: the communication
> Of the dead is tongued with fire beyond the language
> of the living.

"Her face he remembered as the only comprehensible face amongst all these faces that were as closed, as mysterious, and as mute as the faces of the dead who are possessed of a knowledge beyond the comprehension of the living."

There is nothing of further relevance in the immediate or larger contexts of the passages. If we were to ask Eliot the obvious question about this and other correspondences and if he were to answer that he could neither affirm nor deny, should we not then have an obvious and sufficient answer? Perhaps too obvious and more than sufficient, for it is now a matter of public record that Eliot associated Conrad's *Heart of Darkness* with two of his own poems and said of one of them that the association (i.e., the deleted epigraph) "is much the most appropriate I can find, and somewhat elucidative."

*1956*

# The Intimate Voice

SOME YEARS ago I asked a friend what it was about T. S. Eliot's poetry that had made it so tremendously successful, influential, famous, and so on. His answer was that it is the Voice, and I agreed immediately. If I had been asked the question, I think I would have given that answer. Voice fits the quality of Eliot's poetry. It fits better than Language or Style. There are, of course, the aspects of language and style, but the final effect, the final quality, is that of a Voice.

Right now I do not wish to exalt Eliot above other poets, but rather to differentiate. So I suggest that Voice is peculiarly apt for Eliot — as compared, say, to Style for Yeats and Speech for Frost. Throughout his criticism Eliot has said in various ways that the poet's aim (meaning *his* aim) was to create a poetry which captured not only the manner of contemporary speech, but the quality of the speaking voice. His preoccupation with this markedly vocal quality is shown by the substance as well as the title of the lecture called "The Three Voices of Poetry" (1953). In this connection it is interesting to note that he quotes here, as follows, from the earlier lecture "Poetry and Drama" (1951): "In writing other verse [i.e., nondramatic verse] I think that one is writing, so to speak, in terms of one's own voice: the way it sounds when you read it to yourself is the test. For it is yourself speaking. The question of communication, of what the reader will get from it, is not paramount: if your poem is right to you, you can only hope that the readers will eventually come to accept it." Eliot did not quote beyond the word *paramount* — so, for my own purpose, I have continued to quote from the original context. My purpose is to adapt and to construe Eliot's remark in this way: the poem has communicated with the reader and the reader has accepted the poem if he arrives at a point of recognizing a truly achieved voice in the poem. If the reader accepts the poem in this way, then he partakes of or shares the voice which the poet has achieved.

In still another lecture, "The Music of Poetry" (1942), Eliot said: "No poetry, of course, is ever exactly the same speech that the poet talks and hears: but it has to be in such a relation to the speech of his time that the listener or reader can say 'that is how I should talk if I could talk poetry.'" This implies a poetry that is beyond the common speech in the respect that it achieves the very essence of a voice. In the lecture Eliot went on to say: "This is the reason why the best contemporary poetry can give us a feeling of excitement and a sense of fulfilment different from any sentiment aroused by even very much greater poetry of a past age." Like so many of Eliot's critical dicta, this remark has a special relevance to his own poetry. In these remarks the emphasis is on a relationship between the poetry and the reader which is, indeed, an identification. From the very first (and especially at first — in the early poems) the voice of Eliot's poetry was the voice of Eliot's reader. The poetry gave Eliot's reader a feeling of excitement and a sense of fulfillment different not only from poets of the past but from other poets of the present. No other poet had given voice so truly to the deepest and most intimate qualities of the modern sensibility — and it is my impression that no poet of our century has equaled Eliot in this particular respect. There are other things for poets to do and other things that poets have done, but it is Eliot who has achieved for the modern reader the effects of intimacy or identification —

> . . . music heard so deeply
> That it is not heard at all, but you are the music
> While the music lasts.

In this passage from *The Dry Salvages* the use of the second-person pronoun marks Eliot's characteristic evocation of an experience that is at once an intimate experience and also a common human experience — common in the sense of human rather than of commonplace. Curiously enough (meaning naturally enough), an especially good example of the effect of intimacy also includes references to music and to the common:

> I keep my countenance,
> I remain self-possessed
> Except when a street piano, mechanical and tired
> Reiterates some worn-out common song
> With the smell of hyacinths across the garden
> Recalling things that other people have desired.

This passage from "Portrait of a Lady" does in fact present a mixing of the intimate and the commonplace. It implies that there is an abiding essence of the genuine in the trite and overfamiliar — and in this regard we may observe that some of Eliot's poems have had a success so extreme that they partake of a quality like that of "some worn-out common song."

I have said in effect that in Eliot's poetry we find the intimate voice of the modern sensibility, and I would also observe that, like *intimate* and *voice*, the words *modern* and *sensibility* are essential features. The word (and the idea) *sensibility* is especially relevant. An inevitable association here is the famous theory of the unified sensibility and the dissociated sensibility, but my concern is the sensibility and not the theory. I will suggest that just as intimacy is a pervasive quality of the poetry, so is sensibility a preoccupation of the criticism. In this respect it is interesting to recall Yeats's description of Eliot as "working without apparent imagination." By comparison with Yeats himself, this is largely true. Eliot's criticism makes little reference to the imagination and much to the sensibility. The sensibility is more intimate than the imagination. In Yeats's poetry the sensibility is at the service of the imagination, but in Eliot's the imagination is at the service of the sensibility. This difference could be stated in a variety of ways, as for example: in their poetry Yeats and Eliot are both dramatic, but Yeats is dramatic in the ceremonial aspect, while Eliot is dramatic in the experiential aspect.

Another way of making my point is to say that Eliot's poetry is realistic — in the sense that it is a re-creation of the experience of the sensibility. In the third section of *Ash Wednesday*, as in so much of Eliot's poetry, there is an expression by which the poetry turns upon itself and declares itself (and, intimately, the poet). I refer to "stops and steps of the mind over the third stair." From "Prufrock" to *Four Quartets*, the intimate voice presents such "stops and steps of the mind," the states of awareness and the movements from one awareness to another.

> . . . My words echo
> Thus, in your mind.
> *Burnt Norton*

*1965*

# Images of Awareness

IT IS my intention to consider the poetry of T. S. Eliot according to a conventional mode of analysis, but with the hope of arriving at a fresh, or at least refreshed, awareness of the quality of the poetry. What I have in mind is the study of categories of images — by images meaning not only the visual but all the kinds of categories of reference. That certain images, themes, concepts, and so on prevail in Eliot's work is a fact that has long been familiar. In his critical prose Eliot gave emphasis to that kind of continuity and interrelatedness of a writer's work. This has been an increasingly conspicuous feature of his own work, and it is part of my task here to consider how details finally fit into a larger pattern.

My use of this familiar method will be limited. First, I will note what images prevail at the very opening of Eliot's career as a poet, and then I will examine some of these images as they appear in later stages of his work — meaning the plays as well as the poems. In offering a list of the images (or categories) which prevail in the poems of *Prufrock and Other Observations* I am admittedly influenced by the larger (meaning later) context of Eliot's work:

1. Flowers and gardens — eventually the rose and the rose-garden.

2. Water images of various kinds, especially underwater.
3. Months and seasons of the year, days of the week, periods of the day or night, the time of day.
4. Smoke and fog.
5. City streets.
6. Parts of the human body — especially arms, hands and fingers, legs and feet.
7. Human hair.
8. Stairs.
9. Images of music.
10. Images of smell.

The list is obviously not coordinate in an absolute and objective sense, but it is coordinate enough with respect to Eliot's poetry, and therefore enough for my purpose. Someone else might make a slightly different list, with alterations or extensions. For example, instead of stairs, or in addition, one might include houses and all their parts: rooms, doors, windows, floors, and so on. There may be other possibilities, but I believe that my list is essentially valid. There is one kind of image which I did not put in the list and which I mention separately because it is not coordinate with the others: this is the mind, or the awareness, for which all the other images exist.

Flowers and water are placed first on the list because I have discussed them in the past at some length. In order to illustrate the merging of images, I have quoted the lines from "Marina" where these two kinds of images, as well as others, are merged.

> Whispers and small laughter between leaves and
>     hurrying feet
> Under sleep, where all the waters meet.

Another example of such merging is to be seen in these lines from *The Waste Land*:

> A woman drew her long black hair out tight
> And fiddled whisper music on those strings . . .

More common than such merging is the close association of several kinds of imagery. Any few lines from "Preludes" provide an example, especially the following:

> The morning comes to consciousness
> Of faint stale smells of beer
> From the sawdust-trampled street
> With all its muddy feet that press
> To early coffee-stands.

Categories of the list present here are 3, 5, 6, and 10, as well as the image of awareness. As we turn to other purposes and other passages, we can observe, if we care to watch for them, how frequently the prevailing images occur in association with each other. The images which I shall examine in detail are the last three on the list: stairs, music, and smell — in that order. Each of these categories of imagery will serve in turn to guide us along certain directions and through certain realms of Eliot's work.

I

In the Prufrock group, the image of stairs occurs five times in as many poems:

> The October night comes down; returning as before
> Except for a slight sensation of being ill at ease
> I mount the stairs and turn the handle of the door
> And feel as if I had mounted on my hands and knees.
>> "Portrait of a Lady"

> And indeed there will be time
> To wonder, "Do I dare?" and, "Do I dare?"
> Time to turn back and descend the stair,
> With a bald spot in the middle of my hair . . .
>> "Prufrock"

> When evening quickens faintly in the street,
> Wakening the appetites of life in some
> And to others bringing the *Boston Evening Transcript*,
> I mount the steps and ring the bell, turning
> Wearily, as one would turn to nod good-bye
>> to Rochefoucauld,
> If the street were time and he at the end
>> of the street,
> And I say, "Cousin Harriet, here is the
>> *Boston Evening Transcript*."
>> "The *Boston Evening Transcript*"

Stand on the highest pavement of the stair —
Lean on a garden urn —
Weave, weave the sunlight in your hair . . .
                    "La Figlia che Piange"

The lamp said,
"Four o'clock,
Here is the number on the door.
Memory!
You have the key,
The little lamp spreads a ring on the stair.
Mount.
The bed is open; the tooth-brush hangs on the wall,
Put your shoes at the door, sleep, prepare for life."
                    "Rhapsody on a Windy Night"

What are some significant features of these passages? In every case,
the stairs are a literal reference. In addition to the stairs, there is
always a person present in a position or in an activity relating to
the stairs. In all the passages the stairs serve as the settings for
arrivals and departures. I take it that Prufrock is contemplating
a possible crisis of decision: having mounted the stair which leads
to the entrance of a house, whether to enter and join his friends
for "the taking of a toast and tea," or whether "to turn back and
descend the stair." In "La Figlia" it is, of course, a man who has
departed, leaving the girl to "stand and grieve" at the top of the
stair. Except for "Rhapsody," each passage involves a troubled
encounter between a man and a woman. This is emphatically so
in "Portrait" and "La Figlia." A troubled relation with women is
intimated by the passage from "Prufrock" just as it is intimated
by the whole poem. In "The *Boston Evening Transcript*" the
relation between the speaker of the poem and his "Cousin Har-
riet" is troubled only by ironic implication. Between the man and
the woman there are no "appetites of life" but only the *Boston
Evening Transcript*. In the passage concluding "Rhapsody" the
man is returning to the solitude of his own quarters, but the quality of sexual anxiety is present here as it is in the complete poem
and in all the poems of the Prufrock group. Another point to be
made about these images of the stairs is that in every case there

is a character, the speaker, whose relation to the stairs includes what may be called a posture of awareness. There is some purpose here in comparing the phrase with its inversion, an awareness of posture. The speaker of "Portrait" says that he feels "*as if* I had mounted on my hands and knees," thus giving the emphasis to a quality of awareness rather than to an actual posture. It should not be necessary to dwell on the passages from "Prufrock," "The *Boston Evening Transcript*," and "Rhapsody" in order to claim that in each of these the stairs serve as the occasion or point of reference for a particular experience of awareness — which is in each case, including "Portrait," a self-awareness. "La Figlia" obviously differs from the others in that it is the woman who is pictured on the stair, but she is so pictured by the speaker of the poem. The nature of some of the verbs in the poem, imperatives and conditionals, shows that the scenes of the poem are arrangements within the awareness of the speaker. The aspect of self-awareness derives, among other things, from the speaker's reference to "my imagination" and "these cogitations," and also from the identification, however indeterminate, between the "I" and the "he" of the poem.

Although, as noted, all these images of stairs are literal, when they are considered together and when it becomes evident that they have certain features in common, especially the quality of awareness, then the images, separately and collectively, acquire something which is beyond the literal. To the literalness of the image there has been added a measure of the symbolic.

In the rest of Eliot's poetry there are a number of images of stairs. These are of varying interest. There are two passages in *The Waste Land* which deserve our attention. The first of these comes in "A Game of Chess," near the end of that opening passage where there is the description of the woman seated before her dressing table, on which are her jewels and her perfumes.

> Footsteps shuffled on the stair.
> Under the firelight, under the brush, her hair
> Spread out in fiery points
> Glowed into words, then would be savagely still.

"My nerves are bad to-night. Yes, bad. Stay with me.
"Speak to me. Why do you never speak. Speak."

And so on. A significant aspect of the image, the footsteps on the stair, is the fact that it is the sole means by which the man's arrival is reported, the only direct means by which his presence is indicated. His presence is otherwise suggested by the woman's form of address, and by the lines which are presumably his unspoken thoughts in the presence of the woman: "I think we are in rats' alley," etc.

The second image of stairs in *The Waste Land* comes in "The Fire Sermon." It is the last reference to the young man carbuncular.

Bestows one final patronizing kiss,
And gropes his way, finding the stairs unlit . . .

The respects in which these two images relate to the Prufrock set of images are obvious enough. They are both literal. One image is of a man's arrival, and the other of a man's departure. Each of the images involves a troubled encounter between a man and a woman. The matter of awareness cannot be so readily and so simply applied to these images as to those of the early group. In the first image, however, it may be noted that the man is, so to speak, kept out of sight except to the extent of his awareness. As for the second image, the relevant awareness is that of Tiresias, who "Perceived the scene, and foretold the rest" and whose voice narrates the encounter between the typist and the young man. For these two, it is awareness which is lacking. He is assured, vain, and patronizing, and she is indifferent. He gropes his way in the dark, and she is "Hardly aware of her departed lover." The groping and the stairs being unlit give this image a symbolic quality. But both stair images of *The Waste Land* have a symbolic inclination also because they have features which can be associated with the images of the Prufrock set. At this point there arises the consideration that if an image occurs frequently enough to become thematic, then it has in a respect also become symbolic.

At the opening of *Sweeney Agonistes*, when the telephone is ringing and Doris knows that it is Pereira calling, she asks Dusty to answer and to make any of several excuses for her, including this one: "Say I broke my leg on the stairs." In itself this image is of little interest, but it becomes more important when it is considered along with other images of the stairs as hazardous and unreliable. These appear in the plays *Murder in the Cathedral* and *The Cocktail Party*. In the earlier play there is the statement "A man may climb the stair in the day, and slip on a broken step," which we shall notice again in another connection. In *The Cocktail Party* the image of stairs occurs in a passage of dialogue addressed to Edward Chamberlayne by the psychiatrist Sir Henry Harcourt-Reilly while he is still, in the early moments of the play, the Unidentified Guest:

> . . . When you've dressed for a party
> And are going downstairs, with everything about you
> Arranged to support you in the role you have chosen,
> Then sometimes, when you come to the bottom step
> There is one step more than your feet expected
> And you come down with a jolt. Just for a moment
> You have the experience of being an object
> At the mercy of a malevolent staircase.

This imagery enriches the subcategory of stairs (as hazardous and unreliable) by relating it so dramatically to the conditions of awareness and of unawareness, and to the experience of a sudden shift in awareness.

The remaining images of stairs are to be found in "A Song for Simeon," *Ash Wednesday*, *Murder in the Cathedral*, and *Burnt Norton*. All of them are symbolic in one respect or another. Those requiring the briefest mention may be noted first. The "saints' stair," in the final strophe of "A Song for Simeon," and "the figure of the ten stairs," in the final strophe of *Burnt Norton*, are both more effectively symbols than images — comparable to (and deriving from) the image of the ladder which symbolizes some aspects of the spiritual discipline described by St. John of the Cross in his *Dark Night of the Soul*. More decidedly an image is that already noted in *Murder in the Cathedral*. This comes in a sticho-

mythic set of lines spoken by Chorus, Priests, and Tempters near
the end of Part I:

CHORUS:
> A man may walk with a lamp at night,
> and yet be drowned in a ditch.

PRIESTS:
> A man may climb the stair in the day, and
> slip on a broken step.

TEMPTERS:
> A man may sit at meat, and feel the cold
> in his groin.

The image here has both literal and symbolic aspects. Climbing
the stair by day, like walking with a lamp by night or sitting at
meat, is a characteristic or typical activity, and as such also symbolic. The image is comparable to Eliot's earlier usages, those in
the Prufrock group, in that the detail of slipping on a broken step
implies the ideas of awareness and of unawareness. The third
image comes a few moments earlier and it is the most interesting.
It is spoken by the Fourth Tempter, the only genuine tempter
because he offers what Thomas himself has desired — martyrdom,
sainthood, heavenly grandeur. In the passage containing the image
the Tempter is revealing his knowledge of Thomas' own thoughts
— that the shrine and the fame of sainthood will decay or be
destroyed, and that the only part of sainthood worth desiring is
the "heavenly grandeur." The Tempter says,

> Your thoughts have more power than kings to compel you.
> You have also thought, sometimes at your prayers,
> Sometimes hesitating at the angles of stairs,
> And between sleep and waking, early in the morning,
> When the bird cries, have thought of further scorning.
> . . . . . . . . . . . . . . . . . . . .
> That the shrine shall be pillaged . . .

The activities mentioned here, like those in the stichomythic set
above, are meant to be characteristic and typical, and they are also
much more highly specialized. While the others are things which
any man may do, these activities have a special appropriateness
for Thomas, the Archbishop. The detail of prayers has a specific

relevance to the play and to the immediate context, but the other details have a more striking poetic quality and are otherwise of particular interest. The stairs, the time between sleep and waking, the early morning, the cry of the bird, all of these occur a number of times in Eliot's work and usually they signify a special moment of awareness. It may be noted that the last three details — sleep and waking, morning, bird-cry — are all descriptive elements of the same moment, so that the image of stairs is the central image of the series here, just as it is in the stichomythic set, and thus the stairs images receive in each case this same kind of emphasis. The clearest and most important fact about the stairs image here is that it is also an image of awareness: "hesitating at the angles of stairs." The Tempter has already said that these are occasions of "thought," and the "hesitating" — along with the detail of the "angle" — gives dramatic emphasis to the nature of the occasion. The image here is, indeed, the posture of awareness, the symbol of awareness, and in so being it relates with marked significance to the images of the Prufrock poems. Each of those images is wholly circumstantial and literal in its own context, but when we observe that they share a common quality, then in their collective aspect they yield the paradigm of the posture of awareness. The image in the play is literal, but also general, and in its generality it is as the paradigm to the earlier set of images. The earlier images have a symbolic inclination, and the later image, by its generality and by its relation to the earlier, has an even sharper one.

We have already noted the image which appears in the opening lines of the last strophe of *Burnt Norton*:

> The detail of the pattern is movement,
> As in the figure of the ten stairs.

The stairs here are strictly a symbol on the order of paradigm, so acknowledged within the lines by the words *pattern* and *figure*. It is this paradigm of the stairs which is applied and elaborated to form the entire third section of *Ash Wednesday*. All of Eliot's images of stairs, earlier and later, are consummated in this poem. As just stated, the activity of climbing stairs is the inclusive symbol. All the earlier images of stairs show an inclination toward the symbolic, and here the symbol is literalized, so to speak, in that the image is extended into a number of details. It is, thus, something like a metaphysical conceit. It is actually allegory, but allegory so vivid in its imagery that we may say that the meanings are not only signalized, but persuasively dramatized. As in the earlier instances, the climber of the stairs is also the speaker of the poem. If there is no troubled encounter between a man and a woman, there are the sexually "distracting" images of the third strophe, from the "slotted window bellied like the fig's fruit" through "brown hair over the mouth blown . . . music of the flute, stops and steps of the mind over the third stair." At the opening of each of the three main strophes of the poem, the speaker is at a "turning of the . . . stair," which is precisely the same posture of awareness as "hesitating at the angles of stairs." Just such "hesitating" is stated in the words "stops and steps of the mind over the third stair." With the reference to the "mind," the image might seem to be losing its dramatic vividness, becoming transparent and revealing too obtrusively the allegorized meaning. But this consideration is made only to be rejected, so that emphasis may be given to the reverse idea, which is actually the truth — for this phrasing about the "mind," with its "stops and steps," produces the most vivid image of the poem, the one in which all the actions and situations of the poem are condensed and intensified. The image is, of course, the posture of awareness. Throughout Eliot's works, the experience of awareness is itself often a vividly realized image, as it is here in conjunction with the imagery of stairs.

## II

While the analogy between music and poetry has always been obvious, it may be said that this analogy was a preoccupation for Eliot. The subject is explored and clarified in one of his finest lectures, "The Music of Poetry." Titles of poems which show the analogy are "Preludes," "Rhapsody on a Windy Night," the "Five-Finger Exercises" among the Minor Poems, and, of course, *Four Quartets.*

My remarks on images of music will not run parallel to those made on images of stairs. But I do wish to indicate that the two kinds of images have a common quality: they are both involved in what I have called Eliot's image of awareness. I shall not attempt to give an exhaustive account of images of music but will attend only to those which relate to the idea of awareness, and not even all of these will have an equal relevance. It so happens that these images appear in some of the poems of the Prufrock group, the poem which is the third section of *Ash Wednesday*, and in *Four Quartets*. The earliest of the Prufrock poems, "Conversation Galante," provides the first instance:

> And I then: "Someone frames upon the keys
> That exquisite nocturne, with which we explain
> The night and moonshine; music which we seize
> To body forth our own vacuity."

The statement is derogatory with regard to the "exquisite nocturne" and those who listen to it — to paraphrase, the music is a particularized representation of the mental emptiness of the listeners. In still other words, the image of the music serves also as an image of human awareness — such as it is in this particular case.

In the poem "Prufrock" there are only two images of music:

> I know the voices dying with a dying fall
> Beneath the music from a farther room.
>
> . . . . . . . . . . . . .
>
> I have heard the mermaids singing, each to each.

It may be said of these passages that in each case the music is overheard. This observation is relevant to the fact that Eliot often indicates the degree of awareness and the kind of awareness with which the music is heard.

"Portrait of a Lady" is the one poem of which music is a prevailing motif. The poem opens with the man and woman having just arrived at the woman's room after attending a concert of Chopin's Preludes.

> We have been, let us say, to hear the latest Pole . . .

With the words *let us say* the occasion is presented as typical as well as specific. The phrase also serves to intimate that the entire poem is recited within the memory of the man, who is the speaker of the poem, rather than simply narrated according to the indeterminate occasion of literary convention. So considered, the poem approaches the kind of "interior monologue" which is fully developed in "Prufrock." The perspective of memory and typicality and the mode of interior monologue are decidedly resumed in the final passage of the poem. Returning to the first section, we note that as "the conversation slips," the sounds of violins and cornets echo in the mind of the man, thus indicating a diffusion of awareness and a quality of strain and distress in the man's relation with both music and woman. Since Chopin's Preludes are exclusively for piano, the shift in reference to violins and cornets contributes to the diffusion of awareness. Finally, to the mingled sounds of these instruments and the woman's conversation there is added an actual headache, which is represented in musical terms:

> Inside my brain a dull tom-tom begins
> Absurdly hammering a prelude of its own,
> Capricious monotone
> That is at least one definite "false note."

The second section of the poem contains two images of music, both of which present music as unwelcome invasions of awareness. In the first of these the voice of the woman is again associated with the irritating sound of a musical instrument.

> The voice returns like the insistent out-of-tune
> Of a broken violin on an August afternoon.

The second image comes in the final lines of the section, at the end of a passage of interior monologue where the speaker describes himself as he might be found reading the newspaper "any morning in the park":

> I keep my countenance,
> I remain self-possessed
> Except when a street piano, mechanical and tired
> Reiterates some worn-out common song
> With the smell of hyacinths across the garden

Recalling things that other people have desired.
Are these ideas right or wrong?

In this passage the speaker tells of one kind of awareness being displaced by another. While reading the newspaper, he is self-possessed, a spectator standing aside from the commotions of the world, of other people — until the common song of the street piano and the smell of hyacinths provoke an awareness of "things . . . desired," desired by the speaker himself as well as by "other people." The speaker loses his self-possession when he becomes aware of the desires which are common to mankind, including himself. This dichotomy between desire and the newspaper is the same as that between "the appetites of life" and the *Boston Evening Transcript*.

The third section of the poem contains a single image of music. This comes in the very last lines of the poem, at the end of the passage already noted as being decidedly in the mode of interior monologue. The passage opens with the speaker speculating on the possibility of the woman's death and on how that event might affect him, and then the poem ends:

> Would she not have the advantage, after all?
> This music is successful with a "dying fall"
> Now that we talk of dying —
> And should I have the right to smile?

The words in quotation marks are so put, presumably, because Eliot intended an allusion to the opening lines of *Twelfth Night*, where Duke Orsino says, "If music be the food of love, play on! . . . That strain again! It had a dying fall." But the music in Eliot's poem is not the food of love. I shall evade most of the complex multiple ironies and ambiguities with which the poem ends in order to consider a matter which is complex enough. With the speaker's reference to the poem as "music" the identity of the speaker merges with that of the poet. "Portrait of a Lady" is primarily a portrait of the man who speaks the poem, just as "The Love Song of J. Alfred Prufrock" is a portrait of Prufrock, and both poems are in respects portraits of the poet. Both poems are concerned with problems of love, including self-love. Each is a

dramatic representation (especially in its conclusion) of an awareness which is contemplating itself, contemplating not only narcis-
sistically, but also

> . . . like one who smiles, and turning shall remark
> Suddenly, his expression in a glass.

The imagery of music in the Prufrock group is something less
than lovely. In *Ash Wednesday* the imagery is lovely, in itself and
in its associations, but it is again an invasion of awareness. There
is one main image of music, and this appears in that passage of the
third section already noted:

> At the first turning of the third stair
> Was a slotted window bellied like the fig's fruit
> And beyond the hawthorn blossom and a pasture scene
> The broadbacked figure drest in blue and green
> Enchanted the maytime with an antique flute.
> Blown hair is sweet, brown hair over the mouth blown,
> Lilac and brown hair;
> Distraction, music of the flute, stops and steps of the
>     mind over the third stair,
> Fading, fading; strength beyond hope and despair
> Climbing the third stair.

This sweet flute music, symbolizing the sweetness of the flesh, is
a distraction, an alternate awareness, a "stop" of the mind in its
effort to climb the stair (which is the spiritual discipline of purgation). In the fourth section there is an imagery of the absence of
music, for "the fiddles and the flutes" are borne away, and while
the Priapus-like figure appears again, his "flute is breathless."

All images of music in *Four Quartets* share a common quality:
in no instance is the music both literally and normally heard. In
*East Coker* "the music/ Of the weak pipe and the little drum" is
part of the imagined scene in which the sixteenth-century men and
women of the town dance "around the bonfire." Eliot relates the
rhythm of this dancing to the complex rhythms of life and death
in all of nature, but I am concerned here only with the pipe and
drum as summoned by the imagination. A comparably simple
image appears at the opening of the third section of *The Dry
Salvages*, with "the future is a faded song." This is the familiar

idea that all times are fleeting, moving into the past, including the times to come. The song is faded in the sense of its being over-familiar, worn-out, and also in the sense of its having faded from hearing.

The remaining images of music in *Four Quartets* are more complex. They are related to each other, and they are related also to some of Eliot's central poetic ideas and most compelling themes — essentially one idea and one theme, one and the same. We can briefly review this point by referring to a familiar passage at the end of the second section of *Burnt Norton*:

> Time past and time future
> Allow but a little consciousness.
> To be conscious is not to be in time
> But only in time can the moment in the rose-garden
>
> . . . . . . . . . . . . . . . . . . .
>
> Be remembered; involved with past and future.
> Only through time time is conquered.

Throughout *Four Quartets* the idea of the transcending of time and the theme of recapturing the childhood experience of the ecstatic moment in the rose-garden are expressed a number of times. In three such passages there are references to music. The first of these — "unheard music hidden in the shrubbery" — appears in the rose-garden passage at the opening of *Burnt Norton*. The characteristics of the music here — "unheard" and "hidden" — occur in rose-garden passages throughout *Four Quartets* and are associated with an imagery of laughing children hidden among leaves or shrubbery. This occurs in the passage under consideration, with the words "the leaves were full of children,/ Hidden excitedly, containing laughter." It occurs again in *Burnt Norton* at the very end: "the hidden laughter/ Of children in the foliage." In the third section of *East Coker* it occurs within a catalogue of related images:

> Whisper of running streams, and winter lightning.
> The wild thyme unseen and the wild strawberry,
> The laughter in the garden, echoed ecstasy
> Not lost, but requiring, pointing to the agony
> Of death and birth.

There is, finally, the imagery near the end of *Little Gidding*:

> At the source of the longest river
> The voice of the hidden waterfall
> And the children in the apple-tree
> Not known, because not looked for
> But heard, half-heard, in the stillness
> Between two waves of the sea.

A somewhat different image of music (because not contained in a rose-garden passage) comes at the opening of the final section of *Burnt Norton*:

> Words move, music moves
> Only in time; but that which is only living
> Can only die. Words, after speech, reach
> Into the silence. Only by the form, the pattern,
> Can words or music reach
> The stillness, as a Chinese jar still
> Moves perpetually in its stillness.
> Not the stillness of the violin, while the note lasts,
> Not that only, but the co-existence,
> Or say that the end precedes the beginning,
> And the end and the beginning were always there
> Before the beginning and after the end.
> And all is always now.

Here there is an analogy between poetry and music in the respect that these temporal arts may, by the completeness of form, achieve (or illustrate) the transcending of time. It should not be necessary to attempt an elaborate comment on this passage in order to indicate that there is a common element in the two images of music: the first is "unheard," and the second is associated with "silence" and "stillness." A final image, in the last section of *The Dry Salvages*, combines characteristics of the first two:

> For most of us, there is only the unattended
> Moment, the moment in and out of time,
> The distraction fit, lost in a shaft of sunlight
> The wild thyme unseen, or the winter lightning
> Or the waterfall, or music heard so deeply
> That it is not heard at all, but you are the music
> While the music lasts.

This image of music is contained in a catalogue of images which are recurrent in Eliot's work and which provide the occasions for, and therefore the symbols of, "the moment in and out of time." But unlike the other images in the catalogue, it has its own logic for the transcending of time, which is in accordance with the idea of "form" and "pattern" set forth in the previous quotation. The image here is striking in still other respects. Like so many of the earlier images of music, this one, too, represents an invasion of awareness — except that this image is better described as an identification with awareness. Such, too, was the earliest image of music, that which bodies forth "our own vacuity" in "Conversation Galante." But this image is, again, striking in its contrast, because the music fills entirely our depths of awareness. Just as the phrase, "stops and steps of the mind over the third stair," is, in its context, a consummation of all of Eliot's imagery of stairs, so is this "music heard so deeply" a consummation of all of Eliot's imagery of music.

In Eliot's play *The Confidential Clerk* there is another kind of reverberation of the imagery of music. The difference here is that music is a subject which is central to the action of the play. At the opening of the play Colby Simpkins is the disappointed organist who has become the new confidential clerk to his quasi-father Sir Claude Mulhammer, and at the end of the play he has decided to leave this position in order to become the organist of an obscure parish church. Throughout the play there is much discussion of music, usually in its relation to special problems of awareness. But since there are so many references to the subject, we shall consider only those few points which are most closely related to the ideas we have been following.

The interchanges of dialogue which are about music are among the most revealing of the play. The first of these, near the end of Act I, is between Colby and Sir Claude. While Colby is a disappointed musician, it turns out that Sir Claude is a disappointed potter — and it is in their identities as disappointed artists, but still as artists, that the two commune with each other. Speaking, of his pottery, Sir Claude says,

> . . . To be among such things,
> If it is an escape, it is escape into living,
> Escape from a sordid world to a pure one.
>
> . . . . . . . . . . . . .
>
> I want a world where the form is the reality,
> Of which the substantial is only a shadow.
>
> . . . . . . . . . . . . .
>
> . . . Do you feel at all like that
> When you are alone with your music?

And Colby answers,

> Just the same.
> All the time you've been speaking, I've been
> translating
> Into terms of music.

This comparison in the play between pottery and music reminds us inevitably of the comparison that Eliot has made in the last section of *Burnt Norton* between "the form, the pattern" of words and music on the one hand and the "Chinese jar" on the other hand.

Another revealing (and extensive) dialogue, at the opening of Act II, is that in which the communing is between Colby and Lucasta, Sir Claude's illegitimate daughter. In the earlier dialogue music is associated with the idea of pure form as represented by pottery, and in this dialogue it is associated with a quality of experience represented by the familiar and recurrent symbolic imagery of the garden — as in these words addressed to Colby by Lucasta:

> And *your* garden is a garden
> Where you hear a music that no one else
> could hear,
> And the flowers have a scent that no one else
> could smell.

Finally, of course, Colby chooses, not the solitary experience of music and garden, but the position of organist in the parish church of Joshua Park — which is also a return to his music, but with a changed attitude, a new awareness.

### III

A famous phrase in Eliot's early criticism is that of feeling one's thought "as immediately as the odour of a rose." Although the theoretical concept of the fusion of thought and feeling is no longer accepted as valid, the phrase remains an engaging one. This is so because the operation and effect of the phrase are actually poetic rather than theoretical. In this poetic phrase there is, in a sense, a fusion of thought and feeling. The phrase is one of Eliot's images of awareness. The image of the rose and the image of smell serve to produce an image of thought.

I have referred to this phrase by way of turning to the imagery of smell in Eliot's work. Such imagery is conspicuous among the early poems, involved in the effects of distress and dejection which prevail. For example, in "Preludes" there are the "smell of steaks in passageways" and "faint stale smells of beer." In "Rhapsody on a Windy Night" there is a catalogue of such images — "old nocturnal smells." Of particular interest are "a paper rose,/ That smells of dust and eau de Cologne" and "female smells in shuttered rooms." The latter conveys the theme of sexual anxiety, already noted in connection with other kinds of images. Eliot expressed this theme in his poetry a number of times with further images on the order of "female smells." There is, for instance, the couplet in "Prufrock":

> Is it perfume from a dress
> That makes me so digress?

In "Whispers of Immortality" there is the "rank . . . feline smell" distilled by "Grishkin in a drawing-room." In *The Waste Land,* in the opening passage of "A Game of Chess" there is an elaborate imagery of the "strange synthetic perfumes" of the woman whose "nerves are bad tonight."

I have delayed referring to "the smell of hyacinths across the garden," in "Portrait of a Lady," because that image requires special consideration. As noted earlier, the passage in which the image appears tells of an invasion of awareness, whereby the speaker of the poem is distracted from his newspaper by the street piano and the hyacinths. These provoke him to recall "things that other people have desired." Indeed, the passage may be read so that it is simply the hyacinths which produce this effect. In any event, it is the evocative fragrance of the flowers which contributes intimations of poignancy to the occasion on which the street piano is heard. In the larger context of Eliot's work, the hyacinths recall the "hyacinth girl" of *The Waste Land* and thus the entire body of rose-garden imagery with all its familiar details and meanings. As an invasion of awareness, the "smell of hyacinths" is also comparable to the distracting "perfume from a dress" in "Prufrock." The two images also contrast with each other, thus representing the characteristic polarities of Eliot's female references: on the one hand the idealized figure ruefully lost and/or poignantly remote, and on the other hand a female presence which is repulsive in its physical immediacy.

Images of smell in Eliot's later poetry (excluding the plays) are for the most part references to the smell of growing things and of earth and sea. I will merely note some of these and dwell briefly on others. There are these in the "Ariel Poems": the "valley . . . smelling of vegetation" in "Journey of the Magi," "the fragrant brilliance of the Christmas tree" in "Animula," and "scent of pine" in "Marina." More impressive images appear in the last section of *Ash Wednesday*:

> And the lost heart stiffens and rejoices
> In the lost lilac and the lost sea voices
> And the weak spirit quickens to rebel
> For the bent golden-rod and the lost sea smell
> Quickens to recover
> The cry of quail and the whirling plover
> And the blind eye creates
> The empty forms between the ivory gates
> And smell renews the salt savour of the sandy
>     earth.

In this statement of nostalgic recall of the delights of the senses, the sense of smell stands vividly in the foreground. In *Four Quartets* the few images of smell are of this kind — smells of nature. At the opening of *The Dry Salvages*, there are "the rank ailanthus of the April dooryard" and "the smell of grapes on the autumn table," both nostalgically associated with the rhythm of the river. At the opening of *Little Gidding*, in the description of "Midwinter spring," it is the absence of smell which is noted: "There is no earth smell/ Or smell of living thing."

Among Eliot's plays, it is the early ones — *Murder in the Cathedral* and *The Family Reunion* — which have images of smell that are more than incidental. The images are, in fact, of great importance, and they are all of the same kind. In both plays Eliot uses the sense of smell to represent the deepest and most intense kind of awareness. In *Murder in the Cathedral* Eliot has the Chorus use an imagery of all the senses, but especially smell, to express its sense (or awareness) of evil. This device is first used briefly in each of the last two speeches spoken by the Chorus toward the end of Part I:

> There is no rest in the house. There is no rest
>     in the street.
> I hear restless movement of feet. And the air is
>     heavy and thick.
> Thick and heavy the sky. And the earth presses up
>     beneath my feet.
> What is the sickly smell, the vapour? . . .
>
> ·  ·  ·  ·  ·  ·  ·  ·  ·  ·  ·  ·  ·
>
> God is leaving us, God is leaving us, more pang,
>     more pain, than birth or death.
> Sweet and cloying through the dark air
> Falls the stifling scent of despair . . .

In Part II, following Thomas' first encounter with the threatening Knights, this thematic imagery is developed with elaborate detail in a long speech delivered by the Chorus. I shall quote selectively, including all of the figurative references to the senses:

> I have smelt them, the death-bringers, senses are
>     quickened
> By subtile forebodings; I have heard
> Fluting in the nighttime . . . have seen at noon
> Scaly wings. . . . I have tasted
> The savour of putrid flesh in the spoon. I have felt
> The heaving of earth at nightfall. . . . I have heard
> Laughter in the noises of beasts. . . . I have seen

Grey necks twisting . . . I have eaten
Smooth creatures still living . . . I have tasted
The living lobster, the crab, the oyster . . . I have smelt
Death in the rose . . . I have seen
Trunk and horn, tusk and hoof, in odd places;
. . . . . . . . . . . . . . .

. . . I have felt
The horn of the beetle . . . I have smelt
Corruption in the dish, incense in the latrine,
    the sewer in the incense, the smell of sweet
    soap in the woodpath, a hellish sweet scent
    in the woodpath, while the ground heaved. I
    have seen
Rings of light coiling downwards, leading
To the horror of the ape. . . .
. . . . . . . . . .

I have smelt them, the death-bringers . . .

In this rhapsody of grotesque and nightmarish sensory images, it is the sense of smell, opening and closing the series, which is the dominant motif.

At some of the most crucial and most intense moments in the development of *The Family Reunion*, the imagery of smell appears as a vivid expression of awareness. Shortly after the opening of the play, Harry tells the members of his family that he is alienated from them because they do not share his awareness of evil and guilt:

    . . . I tell you, life would be unendurable
If you were wide awake. You do not know
The noxious smell untraceable in the drains,
Inaccessible to the plumbers, that has its hour of the
    night; you do not know
The unspoken voice of sorrow in the ancient bedroom
At three o'clock in the morning. I am not speaking
Of my own experience, but trying to give you
Comparisons in a more familiar medium. I
    am the old house
With the noxious smell and the sorrow before morning,
In which all past is present, all degradation
Is unredeemable.

In *The Family Reunion* there are two other occasions when comparisons are made in the familiar medium of smell. In Part I, Scene ii, after an extended dialogue with his cousin Mary, Harry arrives at a moment of unexpected elation — "Sunlight and singing" — which is almost immediately dispelled by his sudden awareness of the presence of the ghosts. He describes the awareness:

> That apprehension deeper than all sense,
> Deeper than the sense of smell, but like a smell
> In that it is undescribable, a sweet and bitter smell
> From another world.

The image of "Sunlight and singing" is an intimation of the rose-garden experience — which emerges fully in Part II, Scene ii, where Harry and his Aunt Agatha speak with shared knowledge of this experience, and of the prolonged suffering which is in contrast to it. Each in turn refers to this suffering with an image of smell — first Harry, with "contagion of putrescent embraces/ On dissolving bone," and then Agatha, with "an immense and empty hospital/ Pervaded by a smell of disinfectant . . ." After such references, Harry and Agatha speak again of the rose-garden, and then Harry is suddenly aware of the presence of the ghosts — the awareness, as before, compared to the sense of smell:

> Do you feel a kind of stirring underneath the air?
> Do you? don't you? a communication, a scent
> Direct to the brain . . . but not just as before,
> Not quite like, not the same . . .

"Not the same," since the restored moment of the rose-garden leads immediately into a scene of recognition and reversal, where Harry sees the ghosts whom he has been fleeing — the Eumenides — as "bright angels" whom he now wishes to follow.

There is an image of smell in Eliot's latest poem, "A Dedication to My Wife," which is on the last page of *Collected Poems 1909–1962*. An earlier version of this poem appeared at the front of the volume of Eliot's play *The Elder Statesman*, where it is called simply "To My Wife":

> To whom I owe the leaping delight
> That quickens my senses in our wakingtime

And the rhythm that governs the repose of our sleepingtime,
    The breathing in unison

Of lovers . . .
Who think the same thoughts without need of speech
And babble the same speech without need of meaning:

To you I dedicate this book, to return as best I can
With words a little part of what you have given me.
The words mean what they say, but some have a further
    meaning
            For you and me only.

In the later version the broken line is completed — "Of lovers
whose bodies smell of each other." The colon after "meaning" has
been changed to a period. The entire last stanza has been dropped
and these lines added:

No peevish winter wind shall chill
No sullen tropic sun shall wither
The roses in the rose-garden which is ours and ours only

But this dedication is for others to read:
These are private words addressed to you in public.

The punctuation after "lovers," indicating a deletion, makes clear
that Eliot considered the entire line an essential part of the poem.
The sign of deletion tells us that the line belonged to the poem
from the start, and that Eliot intended for it to be revealed eventually — and less conspicuously, as it is in the *Collected Poems*.
The line is thus both inconspicuous and conspicuous — and I take
this to be a typical example of Eliot's well-known serious wit. Another aspect of his familiar wittiness here is the fact that the line
is shocking, for the witty and the shocking are sometimes closely
related effects of the same occasion. The image of "lovers whose
bodies smell of each other" is not only an image of awareness, but
of shared awareness, which is the subject of the entire passage and
the entire poem. Such awareness, in being shared, differs significantly from so many of Eliot's images of awareness, which are
images of isolation and of exclusively held intensities. The image
of smell here also differs markedly from Eliot's earlier images of
the human body, especially the female.

The revised ending of the poem is an improvement. In the earlier ending, there is some ambiguity regarding the "words" — are they the words of the play or the words of the dedication? My own first impression was that they are the words of the play. In any event, the earlier ending speaks in effect of public words which have a private meaning, whereas the revised ending speaks of "private words addressed . . . in public" (the words, clearly, of the dedication) — and that is certainly more to the point. The private words about the smell of lovers' bodies are shocking because they are "addressed . . . in public" by T. S. Eliot, whereas they would not be shocking from another poet — Yeats, for example. In the later stages of his career — in the later plays and lectures — Eliot was concerned with changes of attitude and readjustments of position. With the private-public words of the dedication Eliot was, among other things, readjusting the image of himself. The shocking image of the smell of lovers' bodies finds its place in the larger pattern — and we become aware that the pattern, and the shock, are somewhat altered.

*1966*

# SELECTED BIBLIOGRAPHY
## AND INDEX

# Selected Bibliography

## Poetry and Plays of T. S. Eliot

SEPARATE WORKS

*Prufrock and Other Observations*. London: The Egoist, Ltd., 1917.

*Poems*. Richmond (England): L. and V. Woolf, 1919.

*The Waste Land*. New York: Boni and Liveright, 1922; Richmond (England): L. and V. Woolf, 1923.

*Ash Wednesday*. London: Faber and Faber, 1930; New York: Putnam's, 1930.

*Sweeney Agonistes*. London: Faber and Faber, 1932.

*The Rock*. London: Faber and Faber, 1934.

*Murder in the Cathedral*. London: Faber and Faber, 1935; New York: Harcourt, Brace, 1935.

*The Family Reunion*. London: Faber and Faber, 1939; New York: Harcourt, Brace, 1939.

*Old Possum's Book of Practical Cats*. London: Faber and Faber, 1939; New York: Harcourt, Brace, 1939.

*Four Quartets*. New York: Harcourt, Brace, 1943; London: Faber and Faber, 1944.

*The Cocktail Party*. London: Faber and Faber, 1950; New York: Harcourt, Brace, 1950.

*The Confidential Clerk*. London: Faber and Faber, 1954; New York: Harcourt, Brace, 1954.

*The Elder Statesman*. London: Faber and Faber, 1959; New York: Farrar, Straus and Cudahy, 1959.

SELECTED AND COLLECTED EDITIONS

*Ara Vos Prec*. London: Ovid Press, 1920.

*Poems*. New York: Knopf, 1920.

*Poems 1909–1925*. London: Faber and Gwyer, 1925; New York: Harcourt, Brace, 1932.

*Collected Poems 1909–1935.* London: Faber and Faber, 1936; New York: Harcourt, Brace, 1936.
*The Complete Poems and Plays.* New York: Harcourt, Brace, 1952.
*Collected Poems 1909–1962.* New York: Harcourt, Brace, and World, 1963.

## Prose of T. S. Eliot

SEPARATE WORKS

*The Sacred Wood.* London: Methuen, 1920.
*Homage to John Dryden.* London: L. and V. Woolf, 1924.
*The Use of Poetry and the Use of Criticism.* London: Faber and Faber, 1933; Cambridge, Mass.: Harvard University Press, 1933.
*After Strange Gods.* London: Faber and Faber, 1934; New York: Harcourt, Brace, 1934.
*Elizabethan Essays.* London: Faber and Faber, 1934.
*The Idea of a Christian Society.* London: Faber and Faber, 1939; New York: Harcourt, Brace, 1940.
*Notes towards the Definition of Culture.* London: Faber and Faber, 1948; New York: Harcourt, Brace, 1949.
*Knowledge and Experience in the Philosophy of F. H. Bradley.* London: Faber and Faber; New York: Farrar, Straus, and Giroux, 1964.

SELECTED AND COLLECTED EDITIONS

*Selected Essays 1917–1932.* London: Faber and Faber, 1932; New York: Harcourt, Brace, 1932. (Enlarged editions, called *Selected Essays*, were published in New York in 1950, and in London in 1951.)
*Essays Ancient and Modern.* London: Faber and Faber, 1936; New York: Harcourt, Brace, 1936.
*On Poetry and Poets.* London: Faber and Faber, 1957; New York: Farrar, Straus, and Cudahy, 1957.
*To Criticize the Critic and Other Writings.* New York: Farrar, Straus, and Giroux, 1965.

## Bibliography

Gallup, Donald. *T. S. Eliot: A Bibliography.* London: Faber and Faber, 1952; New York: Harcourt, Brace, 1953. (Besides listing all editions of Eliot's books and pamphlets through 1951, this includes books and pamphlets edited or with contributions by Eliot, his contributions to periodicals, translations of his writings into foreign languages, and recordings of his readings. Earlier versions of this book were *A Catalogue of English and American First Editions of the Writings of T. S. Eliot*, 1937, and *A Bibliographical Check-List of the Writings of T. S. Eliot*, 1947, both published in New Haven by the Yale University Library.)

## Interpretive and Critical Studies

Braybrooke, Neville, ed. *T. S. Eliot: A Symposium for His Seventieth Birthday.* London: Hart-Davis, 1958. (Contains contributions by Vernon Watkins, Djuna Barnes, Charles Causley, Rose Macaulay, Harold Nicolson, Philip Mairet, Paul Jennings, Elizabeth Sewell, E. Martin Browne, Robert Speaight,

Alison Leggatt, George Hoellering, Michael Barry, Denis ApIvor, Hugh Din-widdy, Elizabeth Hamilton, L. P. Hartley, Piers Croke, Mary Drummond, Francesca Tolhurst, Diana Steward, John Nicholson, Elizabeth Gordon, W. F. Jackson Knight, Vincent Cronin, J. M. Cameron, Iris Murdoch, Raymond Preston, Stevie Smith, Martin Jarrett-Kerr, Hugo Manning, Isobel English, John Rosenberg, D. E. S. Maxwell, John Betjeman, and G. S. Fraser.)

Drew, Elizabeth. *T. S. Eliot: The Design of His Poetry*. New York: Scribner's, 1949.

Gardner, Helen. *The Art of T. S. Eliot*. London: Cresset Press, 1949; New York: Dutton, 1950 (paperback 1959).

George, A. G. *T. S. Eliot: His Mind and Art*. London: Asia Publishing House, 1962.

Greene, E. J. H. *T. S. Eliot et la France*. Paris: Boivin, 1951.

Grudin, Louis. *Mr. Eliot among the Nightingales*. Paris: Lawrence Drake, 1932.

Headings, Philip R. *T. S. Eliot*. New York: Twayne, 1964.

Howarth, Herbert. *Some Figures behind T. S. Eliot*. Boston: Houghton Mifflin, 1964.

Jones, David E. *The Plays of T. S. Eliot*. London: Routledge and Kegan Paul, 1960.

Jones, Genesius, O.F.M. *Approach to the Purpose: A Study of the Poetry of T. S. Eliot*. New York: Barnes and Noble, 1965.

Kenner, Hugh. *The Invisible Poet: T. S. Eliot*. New York: McDowell, Obolensky, 1959.

————, ed. *T. S. Eliot: A Collection of Critical Essays*. Englewood Cliffs, N.J.: Prentice-Hall, 1962 (paperback). (Contains essays by Hugh Kenner, Arthur Mizener, Wyndham Lewis, R. P. Blackmur, Elizabeth Sewell, S. Musgrove, George L. K. Morris, F. R. Leavis, D. W. Harding, Allen Tate, Ezra Pound, William Empson, John Peter, Denis Donoghue, and Donald Davie.)

Knoll, Robert E., ed. *Storm over The Waste Land*. Chicago: Scott, Forsman, 1964 (paperback). (Contains essays by Hugh Kenner, D. E. S. Maxwell, William Wasserstrom, F. R. Leavis, F. O. Matthiessen, Cleanth Brooks, Delmore Schwartz, Graham Hough, David Craig, and Karl Shapiro.)

Lu, Fei-Pai. *T. S. Eliot: The Dialectical Structure of His Theory of Poetry*. Chicago: University of Chicago Press, 1966.

Lucy, Sean. *T. S. Eliot and the Idea of Tradition*. London: Cohen and West, 1960.

March, Richard, and Tambimuttu, eds. *T. S. Eliot: A Symposium*. London: Editions Poetry, 1948; Chicago: Regnery, 1949. (Contains contributions by Clive Bell, Conrad Aiken, Wyndham Lewis, Edith Sitwell, William Empson, James Reeves, W. H. Auden, Desmond Hawkins, Nicholas Moore, Montgomery Belgion, F. V. Morley, Ronald Bottrall, Emilio Cecchi, Tambimuttu, Kathleen Raine, Nevill Coghill, Lawrence Durrell, John Betjeman, Pierre Jean Jouve, Bishnu Dey, E. F. C. Ludowyk, Stephen Spender, Ashley Dukes, Ernst Robert Curtius, George Seferis, George Barker, G. B. Angioletti, Henri Fluchère, Louis MacNeice, Edwin Muir, Luciano Anceschi, G. S. Fraser, Michael Hamburger, Marianne Moore, Bro. George Every, Anne Ridler, Eugenio Montale, E. Martin Browne, Claude Edmonde Magny, Hugh Gordon Porteus, Amalendu Bose, Norman Nicholson, Ruthven Todd, John Heath-Stubbs, Vernon Watkins, Mario Praz, and Richard March.)

Matthiessen, F. O. *The Achievement of T. S. Eliot*. New York: Oxford, 1935. (Second edition, enlarged, 1947. Third edition, with additional chapter by C. L. Barber, 1958. Paperback, 1959.)

Maxwell, D. E. S. *The Poetry of T. S. Eliot.* London: Routledge and Kegan Paul, 1952.

Melchiori, Giorgio. *The Tightrope Walkers: Studies of Mannerism in Modern English Literature.* New York: Macmillan, 1936. (Contains much material on Eliot.)

Preston, Raymond. *Four Quartets Rehearsed.* New York: Sheed and Ward, 1946.

Rajan, B., ed. *T. S. Eliot: A Study of His Writings by Several Hands.* London: Dobson, 1947. (Contains essays by Cleanth Brooks, E. E. Duncan Jones, Helen L. Gardner, B. Rajan, Philip Wheelright, Anne Ridler, M. C. Bradbrook, and Wolf Mankowitz.)

Robbins, R. H. *The T. S. Eliot Myth.* New York: Schuman, 1951.

Smidt, Kristian. *Poetry and Belief in the Work of T. S. Eliot.* Oslo: Jacob Dybwad, 1949.

Smith, Carol H. *T. S. Eliot's Dramatic Theory and Practice.* Princeton, N.J.: Princeton University Press, 1963.

Smith, Grover. *T. S. Eliot's Poetry and Plays: A Study in Sources and Meaning.* Chicago: University of Chicago Press, 1956. (The third impression, 1960, is enlarged, paperback.)

Tate, Allen, ed. "T. S. Eliot (1888–1965)," a special issue of *Sewanee Review,* Vol. 74, No. 1 (January–March 1966). (Contains articles by I. A. Richards, Sir Herbert Read, Stephen Spender, Bonamy Dobrée, Ezra Pound, Frank Morley, C. Day Lewis, E. Martin Browne, Helen Gardner, Robert Speaight, Conrad Aiken, Leonard Unger, Frank Kermode, Robert Richman, G. Wilson Knight, Mario Praz, Austin Warren, Wallace Fowlie, Cleanth Brooks, Janet Adam Smith, Robert Giroux, Francis Noel Lees, H. S. Davies, B. Rajan, Neville Braybrooke, and Allen Tate, in addition to Eliot's essay "American Literature and the American Language.")

Thompson, Eric. *T. S. Eliot: The Metaphysical Perspective.* Carbondale: Southern Illinois University Press, 1963.

Unger, Leonard, ed. *T. S. Eliot: A Selected Critique.* New York: Rinehart, 1948; reissued New York: Russell and Russell, 1966. (Contains essays by Conrad Aiken, Richard Aldington, E. M. Forster, Ezra Pound, Mark Van Doren, Paul Elmer More, Malcolm Cowley, Granville Hicks, Harold J. Laski, Delmore Schwartz, John Crowe Ransom, Yvor Winters, Van Wyck Brooks, Ferner Nuhn, D. S. Savage, Karl Shapiro, T. H. Thompson, Edmund Wilson, F. R. Leavis, I. A. Richards, F. O. Matthiessen, R. P. Blackmur, Stephen Spender, William Butler Yeats, Allen Tate, Mario Praz, Cleanth Brooks, Leonard Unger, James Johnson Sweeney, C. L. Barber, and Louis L. Martz.)

Williamson, George. *A Reader's Guide to T. S. Eliot.* New York: Noonday Press, 1953 (paperback, 1957).

Williamson, Hugh Ross. *The Poetry of T. S. Eliot.* New York: Putnam, 1933.

# Index

*Achievement of T. S. Eliot, The* (Matthiessen), 93–97, 122
Adams, Henry, 99
*Aeneid, The*, 66
*After Strange Gods* (Eliot), 39
Aiken, Conrad, 101
Aldington, Richard, 93
*Alice in Wonderland* (Carroll), 151
"Amy Foster" (Conrad), 156
"Animula" (Eliot), 105–106
*Appearance and Reality* (Bradley), 16
"Ariel Poems" (Eliot), 23, 24, 180
*Art of T. S. Eliot, The* (Gardner), 151
*Ascent of Mount Carmel, The* (St. John of the Cross), 42
*Ash Wednesday* (Eliot), 3–4, 6, 12, 17–18, 23–26, 28, 32–34, 41–68, 74, 76–79, 86–87, 93, 101, 114, 160, 167, 169–171, 174, 180
*Athenaeum*, 144
"Autre Complainte de Lord Pierrot" (Laforgue), 10
*Ave Maria*, 48, 106
*Axel's Castle* (Wilson), 101

*Baghavad Gita*, 120
Barber, C. L., 84, 86, 101
*Bartlett's Familiar Quotations*, 153
Baudelaire, Charles Pierre, 10, 42, 75, 142
*Beast in the Jungle, The* (James), 12

Bible, 118, 142, 154
Blackmur, R. P., 97
Bodkin, Maud, 101
"*Boston Evening Transcript, The*" (Eliot), 163–165, 173
Bradley, F. H., 8, 16, 63
Brooks, Cleanth, 3–4, 41, 58, 72, 75, 101
Brooks, Van Wyck, 99
*Burnt Norton* (Eliot), 26–28, 32, 34, 43, 45, 51, 55–56, 60–62, 66, 79–83, 86–87, 90, 115, 119, 125, 130, 139–141, 152–153, 160, 167, 169, 175–176, 178
*Bussy d'Ambois* (Chapman), 117
Byron, George Gordon, Lord, 10, 20

Cavalcanti, Guido, 24, 44, 47, 49
Chapman, George, 117
Chopin, Frédéric François, 171–172
*Cocktail Party, The* (Eliot), 14, 29–30, 116, 119, 127–128, 135–139, 167
*Collected Poems 1909–1935* (Eliot), 25, 31, 140
*Collected Poems 1909–1962* (Eliot), 183–184
Colossians, 60
*Confidential Clerk, The* (Eliot), 12, 14, 30, 32, 116, 127–129, 136–140, 177–178
Conrad, Joseph, 5, 22, 108–156
"Conversation Galante" (Eliot), 10–11, 171, 177
"Coriolan" (Eliot), 24–25

193

Cowley, Malcolm, 99
*Criterion*, 8
"Cultivation of Christmas Trees, The" (Eliot), 23

Daiches, David, 99
Daniel, Arnaut, 60
"Dans le Restaurant" (Eliot), 23, 32, 70–73, 75–76
Dante, 44–45, 49–50, 59–61, 67, 69–71, 77, 80, 94, 142–143
*Dark Night of the Soul, The* (St. John of the Cross), 33, 42–48, 51, 56–57, 67, 76, 81, 86–87, 167
"Dedication to My Wife, A" (Eliot), 31, 183–185
De Voto, Bernard, 100
*Divine Comedy, The* (Dante), 50
Dobrée, Bonamy, 96
Donne, John, 36, 54, 153–154
Drew, Elizabeth, 108
*Dry Salvages, The* (Eliot), 27–28, 88–90, 115, 120–124, 139–140, 159, 174, 176, 180

*East Coker* (Eliot), 26–28, 34, 37, 87–89, 139–141, 174–175
"*East Coker*: A Reading" (Sweeney), 87
Eastman, Max, 101
Ecclesiastes, 154–155
*Egoist*, 8
*Elder Statesman, The* (Eliot), 15, 30, 183–184
Elijah, 51
Eliot, Henry Ware, 8
"Eliot and the Plain Reader" (Stonier), 97
"Eliot's 'Game of Chess' and Conrad's 'The Return'" (Morris), 154
Elyot, Sir Thomas, 140
*Encyclopedia of Religion and Ethics*, 53
Ephesians, 60
"Experience and the Objects of Knowledge in the Philosophy of F. H. Bradley" (Eliot), 16
Ezekiel, 51–52

*Family Reunion, The* (Eliot), 12–14, 16, 26, 32, 38, 82–87, 96, 101, 108, 116, 119, 120, 126, 132–137, 139, 152, 181–183
Fergusson, Francis, 99, 101

"Figlia che Piange, La" (Eliot), 11, 32, 72, 106–107, 131, 164–165
"Five-Finger Exercises" (Eliot), 170
Fletcher, Valerie (Mrs. T. S. Eliot), 9
Forster, E. M., 100
*Four Quartets* (Eliot), 6, 12, 26–28, 34, 37, 77, 87–91, 96, 101, 107, 125, 135, 139–141, 160, 170–171, 174–177, 180
*From Ritual to Romance* (Weston), 42
Frost, Robert, 157
"Fusion and Experience" (Unger), 6

Gardner, Helen, 101, 151
Genesis, 53
"Gerontion" (Eliot), 10, 17, 21–22, 34, 39, 74–75, 81
Goethe, Johann Wolfgang von, 38
*Gog-Magog*, 97
Greene, E. J. H., 107–108
Grimm, Jakob, 50–51, 53
Grudin, Louis, 94

Hadrian, 106–107
Haigh-Wood, Vivienne Haigh (Mrs. T. S. Eliot), 8
Hall, Donald, 7
"Hamlet" (Laforgue), 5, 103–107, 112–117, 142
*Hamlet* (Shakespeare), 36–37
"Hamlet and His Problems" (Eliot), 36
Hartley, David, 117
*Harvard Advocate*, 8, 10, 11
"Harvard Exiles, The" (Wecter), 99
*Heart of Darkness* (Conrad), 5, 22, 108–145
Hicks, Granville, 99
*Hollow Men, The* (Eliot), 17, 23, 25–26, 34, 104–105, 108, 112–114
Horace, 143
"Hysteria" (Eliot), 11

James, Henry, 12–13, 99
John (apostle), 62
John of the Cross, St., 3, 33–34, 42–44, 46–48, 51, 54, 56, 60, 63, 67, 76, 81, 86–87, 142, 167
"Jolly Corner, The" (James), 13
Jonson, Ben, 143
"Journey of the Magi" (Eliot), 51, 147, 180

Joyce, James, 108
"Juniper Tree, The" (Grimm), 50, 53

Kipling, Rudyard, 38, 143–144, 151
"Kipling Redivivus" (Eliot), 144

Laforgue, Jules, 5, 10–12, 103–107, 112–
117, 132–133, 135, 141–142
Laski, Harold J., 92, 99
Lawrence, D. H., 151
Leavis, F. R., 60–61, 93, 97, 101
Letters of Ezra Pound, The, 108
Lewis, Wyndham, 94
Literary Fallacy, The (De Voto), 100
Little Gidding (Eliot), 29, 39, 90–91,
139–140, 155–156, 181
Lord Jim (Conrad), 144–145
"Love Song of J. Alfred Prufrock, The"
(Eliot), 11, 13, 16–17, 19–21, 33, 73,
160, 163–165, 171–173, 180

Mallarmé, Stéphane, 10
Man in the Name, The (Unger), 6
Mangan, Sherry, 97
"Marina" (Eliot), 33, 51, 59, 78, 162,
180
Martz, Louis L., 101, 151
Marx, Karl, 39
Matthiessen, F. O., 93–97, 122
Meditations (Donne), 153–154
"Metaphysical Poets, The" (Eliot), 35
Micah, 63
Milton, John, 38
Modern Language Notes, 154
Modern Poetry and the Tradition
(Brooks), 72
Moralités Légendaires (Laforgue), 103
More, Paul Elmer, 93–95
Morris, R. L., 154
Murder in the Cathedral (Eliot), 14, 26,
96, 101, 107–108, 115, 119, 125–126,
132–134, 139, 167–170, 181
"Music of Poetry, The" (Eliot), 117,
158, 171

New Bearings in English Poetry (Leav-
is), 97
Newman, Francis, 5
Nuhn, Ferner, 99

Outcast of the Islands, An (Conrad),
148–151

"Outpost of Progress, An" (Conrad),
146–148, 150, 154

Pagany, 97
Paradiso (Dante), 50, 60, 62, 80
Paris Review, 7, 36
Parsons, I. M., 98
Peacock, Ronald, 96
Pericles (Shakespeare), 33, 78, 79
Poems 1920 (Eliot), 25, 39, 70
Poet in the Theatre, The (Peacock), 96
"Poetry and Drama" (Eliot), 38, 134,
157–158
"Portrait of a Lady" (Eliot), 11–13, 32,
73, 159, 163–165, 171–174, 179
Pound, Ezra, 22–23, 108
Praz, Mario, 49, 58
"Preludes" (Eliot), 20, 113–114, 119,
162–163, 170, 179
Preston, Raymond, 101
Prufrock and Other Observations
(Eliot), 10, 17, 31, 161, 163, 166–167,
169, 171, 174
Purgatorio (Dante), 45, 50, 56, 58

Ransom, John Crowe, 3, 94, 98
"Return, The" (Conrad), 153–154
"Rhapsody on a Windy Night" (Eliot),
164–165, 170, 179
Rock, The (Eliot), 45, 108, 115, 118, 121
Rossetti, D. G., 44, 50

Sacred Wood, The (Eliot), 93
St. John of the Cross, see John of the
Cross
Santayana, George, 99
Savage, D. S., 94, 99
Savonarola, Girolamo, 8
Schwartz, Delmore, 100
Selected Essays (Eliot), 16
Seneca, 117
"Shadow in the Rose Garden, The"
(Lawrence), 151
Shadow-Line, The (Conrad), 151–153,
155
Shakespeare, William, 33, 36, 46, 78, 143
Shapiro, Leo, 101
Shelley, Percy Bysshe, 20
"Snow White" (Grimm), 53
"Som de l'Ecscalina" (Eliot), 55
"Song for Simeon, A" (Eliot), 51, 56, 167
Southern Review, 84, 87

Spender, Stephen, 100
"Spleen" (Eliot), 11, 16
*Stanzas of the Soul* (St. John of the Cross), 42
Stearns, Charlotte Chauncey (Mrs. H. W. Eliot), 8
Stonier, G. W., 97
Strachey, John, 99
Sweeney, James Johnson, 87, 101
*Sweeney Agonistes* (Eliot), 24–25, 119, 147–148, 166–167
Swinburne, Algernon Charles, 10, 108, 144
"Swinburne as Poet" (Eliot), 108, 144
Swinnerton, Frank, 94, 97
*Symbolist Movement in Literature, The* (Symons), 5, 10, 104
Symons, Arthur, 5, 10, 104

*Tales of Unrest* (Conrad), 155
Tennyson, Alfred, 38
"They" (Kipling), 151
*T. S. Eliot: A Selected Critique* (Unger), 4, 72, 84, 87, 92
*T. S. Eliot: The Design of His Poetry* (Drew), 108
"T. S. Eliot after Strange Gods" (Barber), 84
"T. S. Eliot and His Impersonal Theory of Art" (Fergusson), 99–100
*T. S. Eliot et la France* (Greene), 108
"Thoughts after Lambeth" (Eliot), 37, 60
"Three Voices of Poetry, The" (Eliot), 141, 157–158
*Time*, 101
"To My Wife" (Eliot), 183–185

"Tradition and the Individual Talent" (Eliot), 17, 35, 142
*Tristan and Isolde* (Wagner), 75
*Twelfth Night* (Shakespeare), 173

*Use of Poetry and the Use of Criticism, The* (Eliot), 117–118, 125

Villon, François, 143
Virgil, 38, 143
*Vita Nuova, La* (Dante), 50, 59, 69–70

Warren, Robert Penn, 4
*Waste Land, The* (Eliot), 3, 5, 11, 13–14, 16–19, 21–23, 25–26, 32, 34–35, 37–38, 41–42, 44, 51–52, 55, 58–59, 64, 72–73, 75–77, 93–94, 100–101, 104–114, 130, 132, 148–151, 153–154, 162, 165–166, 179–180
Wecter, Dixon, 99
West, Rebecca, 98
Weston, Jessie L., 42
"Wheel and the Point, The" (Martz), 151
Wheelwright, Philip, 101
"Whispers of Immortality" (Eliot), 179
Whitman, Walt, 20, 118
Williamson, George, 93–94, 96
Williamson, H. Ross, 93, 96
Wilson, Edmund, 101
Winters, Yvor, 94, 97
Wordsworth, William, 39

*Years Between, The* (Kipling), 144
Yeats, W. B., 92–93, 157, 159–160, 185
*Youth* (Conrad), 154–155